United States Dept. of State

Cereals of Europe, India and Algeria

Reports from the consuls of the United States in answer to a circular from

the Department of state

United States Dept. of State

Cereals of Europe, India and Algeria
Reports from the consuls of the United States in answer to a circular from the Department of state

ISBN/EAN: 9783337291921

Printed in Europe, USA, Canada, Australia, Japan

Cover: Foto ©Andreas Hilbeck / pixelio.de

More available books at **www.hansebooks.com**

CEREALS

OF

EUROPE, INDIA, AND ALGERIA.

REPORTS FROM THE CONSULS OF THE UNITED STATES IN ANSWER
TO A CIRCULAR FROM THE DEPARTMENT OF STATE.

No. 25½.—November, 1882.

PUBLISHED BY THE DEPARTMENT OF STATE, ACCORDING TO ACT OF CONGRESS

WASHINGTON:
GOVERNMENT PRINTING OFFICE.
1882.

70 A

CONTENTS.

	Page.
Department circular	211
Denmark, cereals of	211-219

Report by Consul Ryder, of Copenhagen.

(Area under each cereal crop on July 17, 1876, 211; quantities and yield of each cereal for the years 1875 to 1881, inclusive, 212, 213; exports of cereals from Denmark, 1872 to 1881, inclusive, 212, 213, 214, 215; imports of cereals into Denmark, 1872-1881, 216, 217, 218, 219.)

France, cereals of	220-229

Report by Consul-General Walker, of Paris.

(Area sown and the yield of each cereal crop from 1871 to 1881, inclusive, 220, 221, 222; approximate showing of the wheat, maslin (wheat and rye), and rye product of France for 1882, 223; exports of cereals from France from 1871 to 1880, inclusive, 223, 224, 225, 226; imports of cereals into France, 1871 to 1880, inclusive, 226, 227, 228, 229.)

Germany, cereals of	230-233

Report by Vice-Consul General Zimmerman, of Berlin.

(Area under each cereal crop and quantity and yield of each cereal for the years 1878 to 1881, inclusive, 230; exports of cereals from Germany from 1872 to 1881, inclusive, 231; imports of cereals into Germany from 1872 to 1881, inclusive, 232; countries from, and seas, &c., through which imported, 232.)

Holland, cereals of	233

Report by Consul Eckstein, of Amsterdam.

Belgium, cereals in	234-238

Report by Consul Steuart, of Antwerp.

(Exports of cereals, by countries, from Belgium from 1871 to 1880, inclusive, 235; imports of cereals into Belgium from 1871 to 1880, inclusive, 236, 237, 238; exports of cereals, by quantities and values, from Belgium from 1871 to 1880, inclusive, 238.)

United Kingdom, cereals of	239-244

Report by Consul-General Merritt, of London.

(Area under each cereal crop from 1872 to 1881, inclusive, 239; quantities and yield of each cereal for each year from 1872 to 1881, inclusive, 240; exports of breadstuffs from 1872 to 1881, inclusive, 241; imports of cereals into Great Britain from 1872 to 1881, inclusive, 242, 243, 244.)

Scotland, crops of	245-246

Report by Consul Leonard, of Leith.

                                                                          Page.
Switzerland, cereals of   247
                    Report by Consul Adams, of Geneva.

Italy, cereals of.. 247–253
                Report by Consul-General Richmond, of Rome.

    (Area under each cereal crop from 1872 to 1879, inclusive, and for 1880 and
        1881, 248 ; average annual harvest from 1872 to 1879, inclusive, 248 ;
        ditto for 1880 and 1881, 249 ; imports and exports of cereals from 1872
        to 1881, inclusive, 250, 251, 252, 253.)
Austria-Hungary, cereals of 254–264
                 Report by Consul-General Weaver, of Vienna.

    (Average annual grain product, 254 ; average annual grain acreage and
        yield per acre, 255 ; comparison of imports and exports, 256 ; pro-
        duction of cereals from 1871 to 1880, inclusive, 257 ; area under each
        cereal crop in Hungary from 1871 to 1880, 258 ; imports and exports
        of cereals from 1875 to 1880, inclusive, 259, 260, 261, 262, 263, 264.)
Austria-Hungary, grain harvests and markets of 265–267
                 Report by Consul-General Weaver, of Vienna.

Greece, cereals of... 267
                  * Report by Consul Hancock, of Patras.

Roumania, grain production of 267–274
                Report by Consul-General Schuyler, of Bucharest.

    (Exports of cereals from 1876 to 1880, inclusive, 269, 270 ; imports of cere-
        als from 1876 to 1880, inclusive, 271 ; imports and exports of cereals
        from 1871 to 1880, inclusive, 272, 273, 274.)
Russian cereals 274–277
                Report by Consul-General Stanton, of St. Petersburg.

    (Area under cereals, 274, 275 ; yield of cereals from 1870 to 1878, inclu-
        sive, 275 ; exports of cereals across the frontier from 1871 to 1880, in-
        clusive, 275, 276 ; exports of cereals across the European frontier
        from 1876 to 1880, inclusive, 276, 277 ; exports of cereals across the
        Asiatic frontier from 1876 to 1880, inclusive, 277.)
Turkey, cereals of:.. 277–281
                Report by Consul-General Heap, of Constantinople.

    (Cereals of Anatolia, Egypt, Syria, Roumania, and Roumelia, 278 ; cere-
   ·   als of Palestine, 280 ; exports and imports at Jaffa, 281.)   .
India, cereals of.. 282–285
                Report by Consul-General Mattson, of Calcutta.

    (Imports and exports of cereals from 1872 to 1882, inclusive, 283–285.)

Algeria, cereals of.. 286, 287
                  Report by Consul Jourdan, of Algiers.

ON

CEREALS OF EUROPE, INDIA, AND ALGERIA.

November, 1882.

DEPARTMENT CIRCULAR.

DEPARTMENT OF STATE,
Washington, May 31, 1882.

To the Consul of the United States at ———:

SIR: Statistics are desired by this Department in answer to each of the following questions, and for each of the last ten years, for the country in which you reside:

First. The area under each cereal crop for each of the years specified.

Second. The quantities and yield of each cereal for each year.

Third. The quantities and value of wheat, rye, and maize exported, and the countries and colonies to which exported, whether by sea or land, for each year.

Fourth. The quantities and value of wheat, rye, and maize imported, and the countries and colonies from which imported, for each year.

As this information is designed for publication in the Consular Reports, you are requested to reduce areas to acres, quantities to bushels, and values to dollars, and forward your report at your earliest convenience.

I am, sir, your obedient servant,

J. C. BANCROFT DAVIS,
Assistant Secretary.

CEREALS OF DENMARK.

REPORT BY CONSUL RIDER, OF COPENHAGEN.

1.—*The area under each cereal crop in the kingdom of Denmark on July* 17, 1876.

[Statistics for the other years cannot be obtained.]

Cereal.	Area sown.	Quantity sown.
	Acres.	*Bushels.*
Wheat	157, 192	421, 300
Rye	644, 059	1, 791, 892
Barley	782, 859	2, 221, 220
Oats	968, 108	3, 986, 876
Buckwheat	55, 761	80, 064
Peas, &c	92, 088	288, 952
Mixed seeds	123, 833	418, 936

70 A——1

CEREALS OF DENMARK.

2.—Quantities and yield of each cereal

Years.	Wheat.		Rye.		Barley.	
	Bushels.	Value.	Bushels.	Value.	Bushels.	Value.
1875	4,695,2?8	$5,240,394	16,839,276	$14,044,557	23,242,716	$18,676,486
1876	4,098,672	4,919,432	14,516,936	13,206,631	18,944,800	15,878,041
1877	4,002,704	5,642,357	15,962,928	11,907,233	19,935,720	15,731,416
1878	5,447,064	5,345,202	17,271,300	11,469,211	24,047,296	16,249,659
1879	5,038,844	5,859,223	14,557,088	10,927,785	20,468,384	15,054,807
1880	5,598,008	6,237,738	18,119,472	18,166,661	24,955,752	19,401,037
1881	3,143,928	3,597,363	16,618,960	15,063,542	21,548,564	15,726,498

3.—Exports of Cereals from

Year.	Countries exported to—	Wheat.				Barley.	
		Unground.	Value.	Ground.	Value.	Unground.	Value.
		Bushels.		Pounds.		Bushels.	
1872	Iceland and Faroe Islands	78	....	117,244	....	17,604	....
	Norway	89,260	....	3,244,940	....	1,104,936	....
	Sweden	2,664	....	22,273,292	....	87,208	....
	Russia	800	....	8,144	....	6,268	....
	Germany	308,476	....	602,593	....	645,556	....
	Great Britain and Ireland	1,124,144	....	18,496,049	....	3,374,432	....
	Holland	13,720	....	78,284	....	68,524	....
	Belgium	234,976	....	....	....	33,608	....
	France	....	....	....	....	....	....
	Other countries	8	....	6,002	....	....	....
	Total	1,774,126	....	44,826,558	....	5,358,136	....
1873	Iceland and Faroe Islands	20	....	204,819	....	12,368	....
	Norway	90,648	....	6,172,038	....	602,560	....
	Sweden	3,720	....	20,696,868	....	90,204	....
	Russia	480	....	43,651	....	1,488	....
	Germany	310,968	....	1,013,912	....	1,210,884	....
	Great Britain and Ireland	530,940	....	19,857,435	....	1,900,820	....
	Holland	60,240	....	461,339	....	35,128	....
	Belgium	382,884	....	....	....	88,468	....
	France	58,560	....	....	....	6,920	....
	Other countries	....	....	11,110	....	59,036	....
	Total	1,447,460	....	54,461,772	....	4,007,876	....
1874	Iceland and Faroe Islands	....	....	303,623	$9,000	18,920	$19,000
	Norway	117,912	$162,000	11,571,902	341,000	835,670	835,500
	Sweden	36,104	49,750	36,426,082	1,076,250	188,724	188,750
	Russia	....	....	620,857	18,250	5,440	5,500
	Germany	155,432	213,750	950,973	28,500	427,632	427,500
	Great Britain and Ireland	363,320	527,000	25,433,495	751,500	2,666,390	2,666,250
	Holland	7,280	10,000	202,200	6,000	13,400	13,500
	Belgium	136,484	187,650	....	....	12,920	13,000
	France	6,400	8,750	....	....	....	....
	Other countries	....	....	4,490	....	65,436	65,250
	Total	842,932	1,158,900	75,522,912	2,231,800	4,234,532	4,284,250
1875	Iceland and Faroe Islands	848	1,000	300,263	8,250	18,648	17,500
	Norway	167,552	204,250	14,131,208	385,500	696,412	840,500
	Sweden	80	....	38,803,661	1,044,750	118,344	111,000
	Russia	2,496	3,000	128,839	3,500	7,368	7,000
	Germany	117,416	146,250	973,821	26,500	454,168	425,750
	Great Britain and Ireland	1,100,856	1,341,750	32,933,525	898,250	2,476,020	2,321,250
	Holland	16,520	20,250	186,120	5,000	75,732	71,000
	Belgium	202,004	248,750	....	....	30,408	28,500
	France	....	....	....	....	....	....
	Other countries	....	....	34,540	750	....	....
	Total	1,007,772	1,965,000	86,991,977	2,372,500	4,077,380	3,822,500
1876	Iceland and Faroe Islands	4,072	5,500	437,054	12,750	10,588	10,250
	Norway	116,612	160,250	22,086,425	638,750	857,232	830,500
	Sweden	10,748	23,000	41,356,700	1,198,750	149,184	144,500
	Russia	....	....	146,813	4,250	596	500

for the years 1875 to 1881, inclusive.

Oats.		Buckwheat.		Pease.		Mixed seed.	
Bushels.	Value.	Bushels.	Value.	Bushels.	Value.	Bushels.	Value.
30, 475, 940	$17, 115, 292	729, 164	$506, 570	1, 839, 316	$1, 931, 591	2, 510, 868	$1, 581, 114
25, 543, 940	15, 540, 586	492, 504	388, 181	1, 945, 100	1, 987, 402	3, 422, 628	2, 544, 609
25, 986, 180	13, 087, 526	987, 204	607, 111	1, 525, 984	1, 420, 625	3, 609, 256	2, 156, 074
33, 133, 724	13, 881, 045	997, 180	546, 171	1, 570, 548	1, 431, 563	4, 384, 748	2, 244, 415
29, 435, 500	13, 093, 086	560, 072	338, 269	1, 363, 056	1, 193, 345	3, 914, 776	2, 140, 643
33, 526, 584	16, 602, 326	1, 040, 564	652, 267	2, 069, 932	1, 971, 400	4, 471, 544	2, 706, 208
29, 524, 012	14, 745, 589	768, 848	510, 119	1, 661, 616	1, 611, 207	3, 820, 948	2, 280, 318

Denmark, 1872 to 1881.

Barley.				Rye.				Oats.	
Ground.	Value.	Unground.	Value.	Ground.	Value.	Unground.	Value.	Ground.	Value.
Pounds.		Bushels.		Pounds.		Bushels.		Pounds.	
3, 926, 908	......	128, 384	......	1, 711, 329	......	7, 156	......	4, 746	......
3, 015, 570	......	1, 527, 148	......	7, 708, 524	......	50, 432	......	......	......
108, 241	......	137, 808	......	3, 965, 698	......	3, 016	......	4, 591	......
24, 108	......	......	......	......	......	......	......	......	......
624, 620	......	857, 184	......	387, 971	......	276, 240	......	4, 699	......
44, 151	......	20, 176	......	290, 062	......	3, 110, 708	......	......	......
495	......	9, 284	......	1, 649, 915	......	......	......	......	......
......	......	9, 724	......	......	......	......	......	......	......
99, 258	......	......	......	53, 614	......	10, 600	......	2, 547	......
7, 843, 351	......	2, 689, 708	......	15, 767, 113	......	3, 458, 152	......	16, 683	......
2, 700, 075	......	105, 964	......	1, 563, 017	......	336	......	10, 528	......
3, 075, 529	......	775, 052	......	5, 938, 915	......	9, 028	......	......	......
381, 608	......	97, 184	......	6, 182, 763	......	46, 864	......	1, 950	......
36, 883	......	......	......	65, 885	......	192	......	......	......
593, 925	......	562, 964	......	353, 980	......	255, 776	......	26, 903	......
56, 533	......	16, 940	......	194, 973	......	1, 948, 016	......	......▼	......
......	......	2, 156	......	859, 724	......	......	......	......	......
......	......	......	......	......	......	23, 880	......	......	......
94, 693	......	......	......	47, 190	......	17, 540	......	991	......
6, 942, 246	......	1, 560, 260	......	15, 206, 457	......	2, 301, 632	......	40, 372	......
2, 691, 401	$78, 750	126, 876	$126, 750	1, 599, 230	$38, 250	600	$590	4, 226	$150
2, 905, 305	79, 250	410, 924	411, 000	7, 883, 803	188, 750	40, 124	27, 500	20, 900	700
357, 601	9, 750	166, 888	167, 000	11, 917, 215	284, 500	2, 420	1, 750	2, 367	75
111, 958	3, 000	......	......	139, 700	3, 250	400	250	......	......
649, 567	17, 750	292, 488	292, 500	248, 631	6, 000	255, 020	175, 500	52, 974	1, 800
72, 677	2, 000	9, 112	9, 000	343, 070	8, 250	1, 181, 164	812, 000	......	......
......	......	......	......	586, 960	14, 000	......	......	......	......
......	......	440	500	......	......	20, 648	14, 750	......	......
58, 791	1, 750	......	......	54, 890	1, 000	6, 720	4, 500	1, 056	50
7, 047, 300	192, 250	1, 006, 723	1, 006, 750	22, 743, 469	544, 000	1, 507, 096	1, 036, 750	81, 523	2, 775
2, 373, 210	65, 000	120, 792	109, 500	1, 650, 302	33, 750	576	500	19, 445	6, 750
6, 809, 376	185, 750	508, 416	400, 750	9, 880, 700	202, 000	86, 844	62, 500	598	25
121, 025	3, 250	79, 280	71, 750	10, 461, 570	214, 000	22, 436	16, 000	2, 539	75
......	......	......	......	24, 684	500	......	......	......	......
729, 752	19, 750	284, 456	257, 750	152, 728	3, 250	90, 264	64, 750	31, 808	1, 075
172, 968	4, 750	25, 280	23, 000	1, 138, 557	23, 250	937, 976	674, 250	......	......
2, 200	......	10, 748	9, 750	165, 330	3, 500	......	......	......	......
51, 780	1, 250	......	......	13, 165	250	1, 392	1, 000	22, 070	750
10, 160, 291	279, 750	1, 028, 972	932, 500	23, 777, 036	480, 500	1, 139, 488	819, 000	76, 460	8, 675
1, 642, 525	50, 250	140, 548	136, 250	1, 818, 936	39, 750	852	500	16, 333	1, 500
4, 573, 215	124, 750	579, 076	561, 000	12, 064, 774	263, 250	9, 580	7, 000	......	......
38, 772	1, 000	36, 620	35, 500	10, 779, 539	235, 250	3, 804	2, 750	5, 017	325
21, 450	500	432	500	......	......	......	......	......	......

3. Exports of cereals from

Year.	Countries exported to—	Wheat.				Barley.	
		Unground.	Value.	Ground.	Value.	Unground.	Value.
		Bushels.		*Pounds.*		*Bushels.*	
	Germany	318,516	$438,000	1,419,620	$41,000	747,988	$724,750
	Great Britain and Ireland	524,306	721,500	61,308,321	1,776,500	1,887,112	1,828,500
	Holland	42,256	58,000	109,813	3,250	28,404	27,500
	Belgium	119,540	164,250			27,820	27,000
	France						
	Other countries			13,904	500		
	Total	1,142,140	1,570,500	126,828,650	3,675,750	3,706,934	3,653,500
1877..	Iceland and Faroe Islands	16		244,490	8,250	17,828	17,250
	Norway	107,893	141,500	17,542,877	588,000	414,656	401,750
	Sweden	24,012	31,500	43,405,512	1,455,000	88,564	85,750
	Russia						
	Germany	234,532	307,750	632,155	31,250	200,452	197,250
	Great Britain and Ireland	147,952	194,250	67,321,884	2,264,750	1,979,348	1,917,500
	Holland			128,480	4,250	4,800	4,500
	Belgium	35,592	46,750			18,060	18,500
	France	72,296	95,000			49,352	47,755
	Other countries			1,806			
	Total	622,290	816,750	129,777,204	4,350,500	2,775,960	2,690,25
1878..	Iceland and Faroe Islands			216,490	6,000	10,508	9,750
	Norway	94,092	114,750	14,579,702	367,750	538,060	504,500
	Sweden	3,652	4,500	41,046,740	1,119,500	98,044	92,000
	Russia					14,632	13,750
	Germany	257,084	311,000	876,543	24,000	319,880	300,000
	Great Britain and Ireland	417,460	508,750	55,700,147	1,519,000	3,795,564	3,558,250
	Holland	122,400	149,250	122,320	3,250	13,680	12,750
	Belgium	132,180	161,000	5,526		35,504	33,250
	France	187,776	228,750			45,772	43,000
	Other countries			18,480	500	7,612	7,000
	Total	1,312,644	1,478,000	112,568,946	3,070,000	4,879,256	4,574,250
1879..	Iceland and Faroe Islands	76		286,840	8,250	8,076	7,250
	Norway	75,764	97,000	11,688,180	333,500	461,116	450,750
	Sweden	44,344	56,750	36,263,128	1,034,250	90,212	80,250
	Russia			4,488			
	Germany	409,760	525,250	858,463	24,500	313,604	279,250
	Great Britain and Ireland	147,264	188,750	49,339,764	1,408,000	4,517,844	4,023,750
	Holland	10,552	13,500	402,736	11,500	60,308	53,750
	Belgium	53,136	$68,000			80,916	$72,000
	France	212,312	272,000			202,476	91,250
	Other countries			882			
	Total	953,208	1,221,250	98,863,599	2,820,000	5,734,552	4,856,250
1880..	Iceland and Faroe Islands	1,204	1,750	250,061	$7,000	9,240	8,750
	Norway	180,908	231,750	15,080,640	425,000	507,104	475,500
	Sweden	136,060	174,250	47,973,922	1,352,000	89,948	84,250
	Russia			1,812,250	51,000	4,916	4,500
	Germany	886,344	1,135,500	766,767	21,500	276,572	259,250
	Great Britain and Ireland	57,600	73,750	51,955,944	1,464,250	4,342,540	4,071,250
	Holland			163,180	4,500	60,052	56,250
	Belgium	5,100	6,500			27,500	25,750
	France	29,564	38,000				
	Other countries			60,709	2,000	12	
	Total	1,296,780	1,661,500	118,063,473	3,327,250	5,317,904	4,985,500
1881..	Iceland and Faroe Islands	152	250	311,820	9,500	17,328	17,000
	Norway	238,332	317,500	11,942,895	363,750	875,872	793,500
	Sweden	220,980	297,000	35,967,190	1,095,250	178,476	161,750
	Russia			257,434	7,750	37,500	34,000
	Germany	274,292	368,500	556,035	17,000	257,408	233,250
	Great Britain and Ireland	6,204	8,250	42,148,025	1,283,500	2,640,968	2,393,500
	Holland			37,205	1,250	32,536	29,500
	Belgium					46,624	42,350
	France					48,340	43,750
	Other countries			9,317	250	52	
	Total	737,960	991,500	91,229,921	2,778,250	4,135,104	3,748,500

	Barley.				Rye.				Oats.	
	Ground.	Value.	Unground.	Value.	Ground.	Value.	Unground.	Value.	Ground.	Value.
	Pounds.		*Bushels.*		*Pounds.*		*Bushels.*		*Pounds.*	
	1,238,298	$33,750	1,021,108	$990,250	158,326	$3,500	375,068	$269,500	3,262	$200
	38,390	1,000	16,344	15,750	4,710,422	102,750	529,056	380,250		
					867,842	19,000				
							15,764	11,250		
	00,669	1,750	356	250	82,511	1,500	1,932	1,500	1,980	125
	7,813,319	213,000	1,794,484	1,739,500	30,482,350	665,000	936,056	672,750	26,592	2,150
	1,710,457	42,250	109,480	95,750	1,390,337	30,250	544	250	7,074	250
	530,185	138,250	150,188	131,500	10,024,528	216,500	5,204	3,500	1,320	75
	180,042	4,500	23,768	20,750	10,736,264	231,750	1,836	1,250	2,918	125
			4,560	3,750						
	492,579	12,250	260,896	228,500	185,180	3,750	110,992	72,750	2,488	100
	319,770	8,000	2,232	2,000	4,920,926	106,250	280,872	184,250		
					863,126	18,750				
	56,140	1,500			9,267		908	750	297	
	8,289,173	206,750	531,124	482,250	28,129,628	607,250	400,426	262,750	14,092	550
	2,242,383	51,000	127,648	99,750	1,767,290	35,000	580	250	6,417	200
	5,366,149	122,000	478,772	374,000	8,686,007	171,750	11,860	6,250		
	237,387	5,500	56,316	44,000	9,072,296	179,500	744	250	2,717	100
	314,090	7,250	204,060	159,500	89,597	1,750	104,028	55,250	630	25
	103,060	2,250	27,944	21,750	6,168,895	122,000	768,636	408,250		
					11,880	250	6,400	3,500		
							33,672	18,000		
	46,057	1,000			15,598	325	800	500	1,140	50
	8,810,326	189,000	894,740	699,000	25,811,563	510,575	926,720	492,250	10,904	375
	2,262,538	50,250	126,812	103,000	2,050,675	39,500	860	500	6,507	175
	3,624,628	80,750	411,924	334,756	6,218,110	120,000	21,716	11,500	67,898	1,850
	49,214	1,000	55,660	45,250	9,234,491	178,500	3,536	1,750		
	998,666	22,250	298,988	243,000	236,703	4,500	396,456	210,750	34,431	975
	154,649	3,500	7,872	6,500	4,170,470	80,750	2,275,296	1,208,750	14,278	400
			7,868	6,500	27,280	500	5,428	3,000		
			7,000	$5,500			130,088	$74,000		
			26,448	23,000			46,604	24,750		
	37,750	1,000			3,113		760	500		
	7,127,645	158,750	944,572	767,500	21,940,842	423,750	2,889,844	1,535,500	123,094	3,400
	2,291,477	52,000	128,356	128,250	2,076,448	48,500	764	500	9,231	275
	3,278,385	74,500	1,280,364	1,280,250	9,018,245	211,000	20,040	12,250	2,384	75
	165,216	4,250	114,604	114,500	9,562,762	223,750	436	250	10,765	350
			12							
	148,353	3,250	724,640	724,500	156,004	3,750	131,712	80,250	572	
	127,468	3,000	27,904	28,000	4,208,751	98,500	908,660	553,750		
			15,220	15,250	475,662	11,250	6,584	4,000		
			8,844	9,000			18,756	11,500		
			96,656	96,750			56,720	34,500		
	47,828	1,250			561		1,504	1,000	961	25
	6,078,727	138,250	2,396,600	2,396,500	25,498,433	596,750	1,145,176	698,000	23,913	725
	2,369,027	52,500	110,616	117,500	2,556,494	64,000	1,840	1,000	6,559	200
	2,522,154	78,000	1,311,804	1,393,750	7,251,547	181,250	13,844	8,250	660	25
	444,631	9,750	341,932	363,250	7,011,402	175,250	4,576	2,750	8,643	275
	2,006									
	230,260	5,000	533,920	567,250	14,960	250	243,036	144,250		
	71,850	1,500	38,092	40,500	4,015,055	100,500	396,184	235,250	14,630	475
			13,000		13,750	592,787	14,750			
							43,308	25,750		
	40,710	1,000			4,070		2,588	1,500	924	40
	6,681,249	147,750	2,349,364	2,496,000	21,446,315	536,000	705,376	418,750	31,416	1,015

4.—*Imports of cereals into*

Year.	Imported from—	Wheat.				Barley.			
		Ungroud.	Value.	Ground.	Value.	Ungroud.	Value.	Ground.	Value.
		Bushels.		*Pounds.*		*Bushels.*		*Pounds.*	
1872..	Norway			3,080					
	Sweden	74,248		181,000		64,948		80,512	
	Russia	113,696		1,936				464	
	Germany	131,112		638,087		20,260		103,966	
	Great Britain	606		13,304		32		2,194	
	United States of America			539					
	Other countries	6,068		344		56		115	
	Total	325,820		838,290		85,296		187,251	
1873..	Norway					64		244	
	Sweden	61,77?		96,881		214,444		426	
	Russia	57,084		220		14,500		264	
	Germany	409,680		489,173		37,492		61,544	
	Great Britain	7,152		19,257		328		222	
	United States of America								
	Other countries	876		57		172		110	
	Total	536,564		605,387		267,000		62,810	
1874..	Norway							5,170	$250
	Sweden	82,628	$113,500	60,119	$1,750	172,628	$172,750	4,203	
	Russia	20,196	27,750	540					
	Germany	350,240	461,500	553,973	16,500	26,596	26,250	47,862	1,250
	Great Britain	6,844	9,500	8,690	250	916	1,000	224	
	United States of America			908					
	Other countries	1,068	1,500	38		532	500	110	
	Total	460,976	633,750	624,277	18,500	200,672	200,500	57,569	1,500
1875..	Norway			90		280	250		
	Sweden	242,116	272,500	43,417	1,250	156,524	137,000	4,400	250
	Russia	412	500	878		4			
	Germany	226,684	205,000	611,726	15,250	29,676	26,000	49,038	2,750
	Great Britain	944	1,000	608		472	500	115	
	United States of America			198					
	Other countries	176	250	869		88			
	Total	470,280	479,250	657,786	16,500	187,044	163,750	53,553	3,000
1876..	Norway			220				1,439	
	Sweden	184,584	230,750	92,615	2,500	184,164	161,250	22,396	500
	Russia	288,388	360,500	178					
	Germany	180,756	226,000	621,152	17,000	31,864	27,750	116,711	3,000
	Great Britain	40,808	26,000	27,270	750	1,744	1,500	127,039	3,250
	United States of America								
	Other countries	80		435		20		356	
	Total	694,706	843,250	741,870	20,250	217,792	190,500	267,941	6,750
1877..	Norway	5,664	7,500			1,608	1,500		
	Sweden	121,108	159,000	61,813	2,000	180,408	160,500	19,340	500
	Russia	119,564	157,000	83,168	2,750	12,124	11,250	130	
	Germany	1,113,748	1,461,750	1,385,053	44,000	205,984	193,000	136,701	3,000
	Great Britain	11,420	15,000	408,635	13,000	24,664	23,000		
	United States of America								
	Other countries	63,516	3,250			208	208	244	
	Total	1,435,020	1,883,500	1,038,719	61,750	423,056	398,458	155,415	3,500
1878..	Norway			1,753				367	
	Sweden	95,036	124,750	77,526	2,000	108,120	86,000	2,704	
	Russia	66,896	87,750	40,405	1,000	7,220	5,750	225	
	Germany	1,236,256	1,048,750	3,794,741	99,500	78,228	63,500	207,401	4,500
	Great Britain	868	1,250	53,687	1,500	248	250	11	
	United States of America	49,708	53,250						
	Other countries	900	1,250	8,837	250	144		10,221	250
	Total	1,460,664	1,917,000	3,977,149	104,250	193,960	157,400	221,019	4,750

Denmark, 1872 to 1881.

Rye				Oats				Maize	
Unground.	Value.	Ground.	Value.	Unground.	Value.	:round.	Value.	Unground.	Value.
Bushels.		*Pounds.*		*Bushels.*		*Pounds.*		*Bushels.*	
24,940		27,097		3,600		25,300			
288,892		317		28,220					
35,464		48,397		540		198,673		1,476	
40				13,172		5,095		6,332	
10,480				1,120					
368,816		78,811		46,652		139,038		7,808	
1,302				6,068					
63,708		220,088		78,868				880	
391,528		402,441							
415,800		99,398		43,316		108,063		11,108	
132						15		113,196	
1,539				844				8,828	
874,158		721,927		129,096		198,078		134,012	
1,904	$2,000	2,640		12,448	$8,500				
2,696	2,500	23,320	$750	141,768	97,500	2,271			
986,420	986,500	1,478		24,932	17,250				
730,344	730,500	94,552	2,250	18,856	13,000	212,341	$7,250	49,540	$53,000
316	250			840	500	770		81,736	86,750
				1,124				23,616	25,000
2,020	2,000			9,292	750			8,860	9,250
1,723,700	1,723,750	121,990	3,000	199,968	137,500	215,382	7,250	163,752	174,000
				118,420	6,500				
10,000	13,500	330		240	31,500	605			
588,176	496,250	1,210		54,380	250				
945,380	797,750	57,809	1,000	20	37,250	172,613	6,000	125,564	110,000
4						168		14,928	13,000
612	500			53,044	3,500	1,650		60	
1,550,172	2,308,000	59,340	1,000	235,396	129,000	175,036	6,000	140,552	123,000
				10,364	7,250				
42,752	36,750	52		134,256	89,500	30,439	1,750	56	
1,483,908	1,275,250	972,972	20,000	400	250				
250,632	215,250	169,351	3,500	11,860	8,250	41,306	2,250	69,008	49,750
						55		138,900	99,750
								268,660	193,000
3,616	3,250	38,385	750	244				416	250
1,780,908	1,530,500	1,180,760	24,250	157,124	105,250	71,800	4,000	477,040	342,750
1,920	1,500			2,500	1,500				
112,864	95,250	32,989	750	455,372	284,250	64,868	2,250	12,432	8,250
1,611,316	1,359,500			90,164	56,250				
906,932	765,500	128,706	2,500	105,416	66,000	20,234	750	48,462	32,250
200	200			1,328	750			519,136	347,250
								1,348,164	900,250
23,552	19,750			480	250	33		12,436	8,250
816	750								
2,957,600	2,242,450	161,695	3,250	655,260	409,000	85,135	3,000	1,938,630	1,296,250
				948	500	370		756	500
12,964	9,750	19,056	250	245,608	138,250	112,609	3,250	2,680	1,750
852,400	639,750	40		80,624	45,250				
1,136,812	852,750	2,362,224	44,250	56,444	31,750	198,577	6,000	30,896	20,500
20				3,600	2,000	5		59,608	39,500
								1,449,712	959,250
39,400	29,500	11,000	250					9,212	6,000
600	500			620	500				
2,042,216	1,525,250	2,392,320	44,750	387,844	178,250	306,543	9,250	1,552,859	1,019,500

4.—*Imports of cereals into*

Year	Imported from—	Wheat.				Barley.			
		Unground.	Value.	Ground.	Value.	Unground.	Value.	Ground.	Value.
		Bushels.		*Pounds.*		*Bushels.*		*Pounds.*	
1879	Norway	172	$250	15,444	$500	20	....	6,899	.....
	Sweden	119,300	156,500	76,447	2,000	140,780	$114,750	23,736	$500
	Russia	74,812	98,250	730	.....	8	....	....	.....
	Germany	625,796	821,250	2,004,408	54,750	31,624	25,500	53,540	1,000
	Great Britain	....	....	11,100	250	1,632	1,250	108	......
	United States of America	116,992	221,750	1,181	......	....	......	......	......
	Other countries	140	250	8,346	250	72	....	10,507	250
	Total	937,212	1,298,250	2,117,656	57,750	174,136	141,500	94,790	1,750
1880	Norway	....	....	15,850	500	908	750	11	......
	Sweden	85,116	111,750	35,134	1,000	171,312	139,250	6,501	......
	Russia	70,924	93,000	627	......	6,376	5,000	....	......
	Germany	575,194	754,750	803,605	21,750	16,828	13,750	133,191	2,750
	Great Britain	4,246	5,500	29,139	750	2,992	2,500	62	......
	United States of America	349,144	458,250	1,430	......	......	......	......	......
	Other countries	9,424	12,750	1,402	......	196	......	358	......
	Total	1,094,048	1,436,000	887,196	24,000	198,612	161,250	140,123	2,750
1881	Norway	....	....	223	......	......	......	......	......
	Sweden	11,469	16,500	54,675	1,500	68,340	53,500	22,259	500
	Russia	109,924	151,500	359	....	20	......	121	......
	Germany	1,527,708	2,100,500	1,241,952	35,250	7,040	5,400	147,345	3,000
	Great Britain	25,472	35,000	131,051	3,750	4,176	3,250	11	......
	United States of America	402,732	553,750	42,768	1,250	......	......	......	......
	Other countries	8,636	11,750	2,419	......	1,080	750	121	......
	Total	2,085,941	2,869,000	1,473,447	41,750	80,656	62,900	169,857	3,500

Denmark, 1872 to 1881—Continued.

	Rye.				Oats.				Maize.	
	Unground.	Value.	Ground.	Value.	Unground.	Value.	Ground.	Value.	Unground.	Value.
	Bushels.	*Pounds.*	*Pounds.*		*Bushels.*		*Pounds.*		*Bushels.*	
	8,712	$7,000								
	19,552	15,000	7,362	$250	111,320	$55,750	150,757	$3,500	2,400	$1,250
	1,775,176	1,442,250			44,508	22,250				
	227,072	185,250	58,151	2,000	12,000	6,000	138,052	3,250	2,296	1,250
					224		198		2,032	1,000
	11,820	9,500							1,338,520	732,000
	1,508	1,500	121		456	250			4,004	2,250
	2,043,740	1,660,500	65,634	2,250	168,508	84,250	289,007	6,750	1,349,252	737,750
					6,404	3,750				
	39,668	37,250	3,487		297,684	172,000	163,011	4,500	5,416	3,500
	1,159,724	1,087,250	660		14,344	8,250	68,905	2,000		
	100,792	94,500	184,682	3,500	10,580	9,500			38,392	24,000
			81,400	1,500	152				58,716	36,750
									3,317,896	2,073,750
	796	750			464	250			2,380	1,250
	1,301,160	1,219,750	270,229	5,000	335,578	193,750	231,916	6,500	3,422,800	2,139,250
	3,200		6,600	250					36	
	12,624	3,250			486,752	296,500	223,028	6,000	2,224	1,500
	204,604	12,500	7,700	300	74,156	45,250			3,020	2,000
	219,880	204,500	100,936	1,750	21,636	13,250	45,532	1,250	22,548	15,500
		220,000			568	250	116		23,100	16,000
									2,386,144	1,655,000
	111,384	111,500	4,400		3,896	2,250			7,872	5,500
	551,692	551,750	119,636	2,300	587,008	357,500	268,676	7,250	2,444,944	1,695,500

CEREALS OF FRANCE.

REPORT BY CONSUL-GENERAL WALKER, OF PARIS.

In compliance with circular instruction from the Department of State of May 31, 1882, I have the honor to transmit herewith the following desired statistics, viz :

1. Statements showing the area sown and the yield for each cereal crop in France from 1871 to 1881, inclusive.

2. Approximate statement showing the wheat, maslin (wheat and rye), and rye production of France for the year 1882.

3. Quantities and value of wheat, rye, and maize exported from France, and the countries and colonies to which exported, from 1871 to 1880, inclusive.

4. Quantities and value of wheat, rye, and maize imported into France, and the countries and colonies from which imported, from 1871 to 1880, inclusive.

French hectares have been reduced to acres at the rate of 2.47114 acres per hectare; hectoliters to bushels at the rate of 2.8375 bushels per hectoliter ; francs to dollars at the rate of 19.3 cents to the franc.

Quantities expressed in kilograms in the French customs returns have been reduced to bushels at the rate of 60 pounds (27.2155 kilograms) per bushel of wheat, and at the rate of 56 pounds (25.4012 kilograms) per bushel of rye or maize.

GEORGE WALKER,
Consul-General.

UNITED STATES CONSULATE-GENERAL,
Paris, France, November 3, 1882.

1.—*Statements showing the area sown and the yield of each cereal crop in France from 1871 to 1881, inclusive.*

a.—WHEAT PRODUCTION OF FRANCE FROM 1871 TO 1881, INCLUSIVE.

[Prepared from information furnished by the French Department of Agriculture.]

Calendar years.	Area sown.	Yield.	Average yield per acre.
	Acres.	*Bushels.*	*Bushels.*
1871	15,871,843	196,571,839	12.38
1872	17,144,575	342,779,814	19.99
1873	16,867,873	232,370,443	13.77
1874	16,987,076	377,757,337	22.23
1875	17,166,962	285,551,418	16.63
1876	16,950,680	270,810,524	15.96
1877	16,910,221	270,330,606	15.98
1878	17,240,612	284,163,284	16.47
1879	17,153,851	225,172,270	13.13
1880	17,001,133	282,250,549	16.73
1881	17,196,944	274,699,385	15.97

1.—*Statements showing the area sown and the yield of each cereal crop, &c.*—Continued.

b.—MASLIN (WHEAT AND RYE) PRODUCTION OF FRANCE FROM 1871 TO 1881, INCLU-
SIVE.

Calendar years.	Area sown.	Yield.	Average yield. per acre.
	Acres.	Bushels.	Bushels.
1871	1, 241, 597	16, 768, 743	13. 60
1872	1, 236, 546	25, 458, 263	20. 59
1873	1, 249, 106	18, 033, 514	14. 43
1874	1, 264, 576	28, 075, 493	22. 22
1875	1, 190, 014	20, 946, 237	17. 59
1876	1, 168, 854	20, 221, 243	17. 29
1877	1, 147, 574	20, 176, 962	17. 58
1878	1, 093, 770	17, 592, 117	16. 07
1879	960, 166	12, 025, 400	13. 04
1880	1, 015, 104	17, 085, 452	16. 82
1881	991, 957	17, 045, 963	17. 18

c.—RYE PRODUCTION OF FRANCE FROM 1871 TO 1881, INCLUSIVE.

1871	4. 694, 617	75, 087, 692	16. 00
1872	4, 732, 620	84, 752, 081	17. 89
1873	4, 649, 556	57, 658, 065	12. 28
1874	4, 623, 703	80, 499, 359	17. 41
1875	4, 680, 028	76, 383, 018	16. 31
1876	4, 541, 690	75, 155, 461	16. 55
1877	4, 562, 881	70, 928, 502	15. 53
1878	4, 459, 891	68, 634, 826	15. 38
1879	4, 374, 526	53, 603, 463	12. 26
1880	4, 566, 930	71, 841, 204	15. 71
1881	4, 391, 877	67, 338, 503	15. 33

d.—BARLEY PRODUCTION OF FRANCE FROM 1871 TO 1881, INCLUSIVE.

1871	3, 137, 723	72, 679, 765	23. 16
1872	2, 670, 721	59, 207, 671	22. 16
1873	2, 709, 535	53, 813, 405	19. 85
1874	2, 713, 492	55, 830, 426	20. 57
1875	2, 579, 631	51, 484, 596	19. 95
1876	2, 687, 208	52, 667, 444	19. 73
1877	2, 032, 577	49, 335, 419	18. 74
1878	2, 497, 143	46, 597, 363	18. 65
1879	2. 537, 817	46, 076, 764	18. 16
1880	2, 600, 519	56, 206, 383	21. 61
1881	2, 530, 301	49, 895, 204	19. 71

e.—OAT PRODUCTION OF FRANCE FROM 1871 TO 1881, INCLUSIVE.

1871	8, 306, 475	243, 722, 231	29. 02
1872	7, 929, 507	230, 197, 872	20. 02
1873	7, 985, 412	217, 840, 852	27. 27
1874	7, 805, 357	193. 907, 401	24. 84
1875	7, 875, 226	197, 210, 382	25. 03
1876	8, 651, 503	209, 227, 222	24. 29
1877	8, 299, 608	195, 724, 786	23. 58
1878	8, 219, 018	219, 309, 777	26. 68
1879	8, 511. 716	210, 717, 187	24. 76
1880	8, 584, 531	237, 755, 476	27. 68
1881	8, 587, 730	218, 191, 231	25. 52

1.—*Statements showing the area sown and the yield of each cereal crop, &c.*—Continued.

f.—BUCKWHEAT PRODUCTION OF FRANCE FROM 1871 TO 1881, INCLUSIVE.

Calendar years.	Area sown.	Yield.	Average yield per acre.
	Acres.	*Bushels.*	*Bushels.*
1871	1,739,252	27,443,469	15.78
1872	1,679,381	30,166,760	17.96
1873	1,707,123	26,167,557	15.32
1874	1,676,383	34,190,233	20.33
1875	1,627,518	25,995,994	15.96
1876	1,631,071	16,753,636	10.28
1877	1,638,531	31,184,662	17.31
1878	1,638,720	32,647,518	19.92
1879	1,550,716	26,019,019	16.77
1880	1,598,978	29,647,432	18.55
1881	1,561,604	30,116,408	19.29

g.—MAIZE AND MILLET PRODUCTION OF FRANCE FROM 1871 TO 1881, INCLUSIVE.

1871	1,688,823	32,230,178	19.09
1872	1,726,183	32,067,160	18.57
1873	1,664,602	27,018,349	16.23
1874	1,606,723	30,584,405	19.02
1875	1,644,043	29,576,651	17.98
1876	1,633,724	20,133,427	12.32
1877	1,636,183	30,380,598	18.57
1878	1,643,964	32,014,590	18.35
1879	1,632,860	22,556,970	13.37
1880	1,660,233	29,291,039	16.80
1881	1,623,051	25,541,478	14.92

2.—*Approximate statement showing the wheat, maslin (wheat and rye), and rye production of France for the year 1882, furnished by the French Department of Agriculture.*

Regions of France.	Wheat.			Maslin (wheat and rye).			Rye.		
	Area sown.	Production in grains.		Area sown.	Production in grains.		Area sown.	Production in grains.	
	Acres.	*Bushels.*	*Avoirdupois pounds.*	*Acres.*	*Bushels.*	*Avoirdupois pounds.*	*Acres.*	*Bushels.*	*Avoirdupois pounds.*
Northwestern region	1,834,777	33,400,707	1,998,628,000	207,563	5,792,935	319,345,000	490,955	10,033,462	546,359,000
Northern region	2,957,388	80,493,633	4,759,623,000	242,595	7,559,699	431,889,000	401,498	10,117,614	552,657,000
Northeastern region	1,399,818	29,985,911	1,783,301,000	52,062	1,119,479	63,207,000	386,948	7,384,145	387,179,000
Western region	2,829,527	43,098,950	2,594,042,000	106,668	3,163,500	123,856,000	342,331	5,810,419	326,281,000
Central region	1,777,035	31,991,158	1,931,745,000	113,687	1,996,561	115,525,000	841,478	14,695,105	793,263,000
Eastern region	2,109,879	38,046,057	2,190,162,000	111,320	2,087,422	118,864,000	417,915	7,909,744	431,058,000
Southwestern region	1,929,565	34,072,589	2,103,975,000	60,859	1,235,417	69,942,500	395,127	5,400,288	313,375,000
Southern	1,318,815	19,354,247	1,060,449,000	44,538	920,017	54,737,100	769,134	13,598,886	743,902,000
Southeastern	1,691,384	16,911,044	1,026,930,000	58,729	560,194	30,507,300	486,515	5,311,520	275,440,000
Corsica Island	84,498	952,322	59,903,000				11,578	101,866	4,098,000
Total	17,872,686	328,306,618	19,517,758,000	998,042	23,435,222	1,327,872,900	4,542,419	79,763,009	4,374,262,000

Wheat.—Yield, 18.37 bushels per acre; average weight per bushel, 59.46 avoirdupois pounds.
Maslin.—Yield, 23.49 bushels per acre; average weight per bushel, 56.66 avoirdupois pounds.
Rye.—Yield, 17.57 bushels per acre; average weight per bushel, 54.84 avoirdupois pounds.

3.—*Statement showing the quantities of wheat exported from France, and the countries and colonies to which exported, during each of the years specified below.*

Countries.	1871.	1872.	1873.	1874.	1875.	1876.	1877.	1878.	1879.	1880.
	Bushels.	*Bushels.*	*Bushels.*	*Bushels.*	*Bushels.*	*Bushels.*	*Bushels.*	*Bushels.*	*Bushels.*	*Bushels.*
Germany	77,880	1,458,500	1,591,200	1,393,900	2,705,000	2,078,600	2,917,400	519,000	239,720	256,740
Belgium	62,610	1,534,100	1,548,800	1,393,200	4,192,000	1,510,200	2,447,000	356,800	233,280	255,900
England	117,080	6,419,900	2,654,000	1,039,500	5,073,000	2,326,600	5,566,000	335,290	42,050	12,130
Spain	5,420	38,140	4,120	38,440	52,200	52,980	7,830	18,020	45,930	11,450
Italy	4,940	38,950	12,580	48,700	4,100	9,190	7,380	460	15,940	13,050
Switzerland	59,890	881,600	858,100	1,168,800	1,643,200	962,900	1,324,700	375,800	225,370	215,160
Turkey										46,230
Algeria	6,110	12,460	10,660	14,530	3,740	3,990	15,950	56,490	56,490	13,670
Other countries	29,670	218,450	164,590	110,840	328,760	288,930	224,700	42,810	86,950	59,620
Total	363,580	10,602,100	6,844,050	5,208,000	14,692,000	7,233,390	11,610,960	1,704,670	945,730	883,950

Statement showing the value of wheat exported from France, and the countries and colonies to which exported, during each of the years specified below.

Countries.	1871.	1872.	1873.	1874.	1875.	1876.	1877.	1878.	1870.	1860.
Germany	$188,220	$2,902,000	$3,580,000	$2,714,300	$4,956,000	$3,989,300	$4,124,000	$1,104,350	$310,800	$505,500
Belgium	140,810	2,921,300	3,404,000	2,566,000	7,212,000	2,782,400	4,870,500	717,100	477,300	477,900
England	234,580	11,651,000	5,584,000	1,912,000	9,980,000	4,441,100	10,843,000	718,480	86,490	26,420
Spain	11,870	72,670	9,080	81,270	104,610	108,130	14,190	36,610	91,180	22,600
Italy	9,080	66,370	22,140	76,900	5,600	13,030	12,010	690	25,130	20,570
Switzerland	128,160	1,638,900	1,757,100	2,064,300	2,674,000	1,677,400	7,455,000	727,400	462,470	436,150
Turkey										108,800
Algeria	12,970	24,950	27,400	30,950	6,800	6,920	36,010	87,710	125,120	29,800
Other countries	76,140	444,700	373,400	213,390	604,500	521,520	450,300	91,140	193,800	103,090
Total	801,830	19,721,890	14,766,070	9,659,110	25,443,510	13,539,800	22,805,010	3,483,430	1,975,290	1,730,830

4.—Statement showing the quantities of rye exported from France, and the colonies and countries to which exported, during each of the years specified below.

Countries.	1871.	1872.	1873.	1874.	1875.	1876.	1877.	1878.	1879.	1880.
	Bushels.	Bushels.	Bushels.	Bushels.	Bushels.	Bushels.	Bushels.	Bushels.	Bushels.	Bushels.
Norway	3,190	769,100	589,300	479,400	432,400	698,700	304,800	13,490		575,800
Germany	367,000	3,443,300	2,473,000	1,495,000	1,196,000	2,680,000	2,384,000	1,382,000	694,700	?,025,000
Netherlands	76,370	344,300	57,940	20,210	121,200	58,780	70,960	9,930		29,030
Belgium	1,655,000	4,216,000	1,843,000	1,362,000	2,526,000	2,923,000	1,811,000	881,800	273,900	1,196,000
Other countries	117,860	1,091,000	897,200	543,600	926,300	1,119,200	774,100	617,900	305,950	386,300
Total	2,219,320	9,863,400	5,860,340	3,900,210	5,191,900	7,479,680	5,354,860	2,905,120	1,274,550	4,213,120

Statement showing the value of rye exported from France, and the colonies and countries to which exported, during each of the years specified below.

Countries.	1871.	1872.	1873.	1874.	1875.	1876.	1877.	1878.	1879.	1860.
Norway	$3,600	$773,100	$635,600	$540,600	$367,600	$633,700	$298,800	$11,580		$649,400
Germany	413,900	3,476,000	2,667,000	1,686,000	1,041,000	2,431,000	2,346,000	1,187,000	$715,300	2,283,000
Netherlands	86,100	346,100	6,250	22,790	105,400	53,330	69,600	8,520		32,780
Belgium	1,866,000	4,237,000	1,988,000	1,536,000	2,199,000	3,652,000	1,778,000	756,700	282,000	1,349,000
Other countries	182,610	1,329,500	1,228,340	761,480	1,014,590	1,387,200	1,067,620	781,350	452,350	636,090
Total	2,552,210	10,146,700	6,525,190	4,546,870	4,727,590	7,157,230	5,560,020	2,745,150	1,449,650	4,050,270

5.—Statement showing the quantities of maize exported from France, and the countries and colonies to which exported, during each of the years specified below.

Countries.	1871.	1872.	1873.	1874.	1875.	1876.	1877.	1878.	1879.	1860.
	Bushels.	Bushels.	Bushels.	Bushels.	Bushels.	Bushels.	Bushels.	Bushels.	Bushels.	Bushels.
England	109,700	30,170	860	161,900	497,500					
Belgium	19,460	112,400	41,110	42,200	65,270	94,620	108,700	579,400	402,400	210,900
Spain										122,500
Italy	74,710	132,700	125,500	210,400	48,460	105,900	221,500	358,100	315,200	78,840
Switzerland										67,660
Algeria										51,210
Other countries	45,430	133,730	93,830	60,250	75,700	68,180	147,700	302,730	893,930	115,990
Total	249,300	400,900	266,300	504,750	686,930	268,700	477,900	1,240,230	1,611,530	617,100

Statement showing the value of maize exported from France, and the countries and colonies to which exported, during each of the years specified below.

Countries.	1871.	1872.	1873.	1874.	1875.	1876.	1877.	1878.	1879.	1880.
England	$129,100	$29,520	$850	$158,800	$463,400					$170,600
Belgium										99,060
Spain	22,919	110,100	41,190	41,390	66,800	$74,230	$85,330	$412,000	$325,000	63,780
Italy										54,730
Switzerland	87,920	130,100	123,000	296,300	45,140	83,100	173,800	234,600	256,000	41,420
Algeria										114,900
Other countries	53,430	131,200	96,120	88,590	70,500	53,430	121,970	222,840	749,330	
Total	293,360	404,920	261,160	495,070	639,840	210,700	381,100	689,400	1,329,930	544,490

6.—*Statement showing the quantities of wheat imported into France, and the countries and colonies from which imported, during each of the years specified below.*

Countries.	1871.	1872.	1873.	1874.	1875.	1876.	1877.	1878.	1879.	1880.
	Bushels.	Bushels.	Bushels.	Bushels.	Bushels.	Bushels.	Bushels.	Bushels.	Bushels.	Bushels.
Russia:										
White Sea	13,267,000	5,629,000	3,317,000	3,650,000	7,541,000	7,570,000	360,500	2,067,600	663,110	11,906,000
Black Sea	1,610,000	374,630	447,030	957,020	70,250	77,420	3,683,000	15,530,260	17,540,400	655,180
Germany	2,995,800	913,950	757,530	1,085,970	50,910	137,270	251,100	2,876,690	2,745,390	1,558,300
Belgium	4,431,000	1,602,000	1,803,000	1,543,000	75,300	322,000	601,540	1,703,520	2,145,800	983,610
England							116,730	1,395,600	1,086,950	224,400
Austria							274,340	598,520	579,390	
Spain	33,480	10,640	197,600	281,500	1,650	2,820	427,350	313,220		1,387,930
Italy	2,148,490	836,360	1,012,410	654,270	426,370	496,360	770,040	1,695,070	700,940	1,135,000
Roumania										1,113,300
Turkey	5,012,000	2,363,000	2,089,000	4,961,000	2,395,000	6,306,000	3,326,910	2,214,710	3,349,700	515,900
Egypt										1,293,000
East Indies								292,670		
Australia	2,811,100	668,440	2,015,730	2,119,640	23,140	483,570	342,740	116,610	855,900	434,300
United States, Atlantic ports	285,400	112,700	367,800	1,910,000	19,700	89,700	634,200	20,163,490	44,533,860	41,102,430
United States, Pacific ports							110,370	361,940	4,051,000	4,677,100
English Possessions in North America								388,160		316,140
Chili	490,000	295,800	300,000	1,489,000	17,900	73,800	2,316,130		790,800	1,327,500
Algeria	1,145,000	2,385,000	3,443,000	2,871,000	1,827,000	3,170,000	57,500	644,140	1,550,980	3,442,300
Other countries	3,088,600	791,100	3,007,100	3,409,700	495,400	827,250		497,600	1,318,370	444,210
Total	37,332,870	15,375,650	18,817,200	29,813,100	12,942,690	19,556,200	12,716,560	51,249,800	81,902,680	74,516,600

Statement showing the value of wheat imported into France, and the countries and colonies from which imported, during each of the years specified below.

Countries.	1871.	1872.	1873.	1874.	1875.	1876.	1877.	1878.	1879.	1880.
Russia:										
White Sea	$24,740,000	$9,006,000	$5,924,000	$14,540,000	$9,900,000	$10,740,000	$377,600	$3,258,200	$1,079 10	$19,073,000
Black Sea							5,916,520	24,478,000	28,561 . 10	1,056,420
Germany	3,005,090	3,627,930	816,880	1,406,760	100,470	118,500	371,690	4,544,650	4,487, 0	2,823,000
Belgium	5,996,000	1,493,340	1,371,490	1,852,810	73,280	204,270	102,000	2,721,580	3,555,1 0	1,575,600
England	8,262,000	1,605,000	3,219,000	2,594,000	98,900	456,400	187,040	2,514,400	1,783,1	483,200
Austria							481,030	1,005,200	1,051,7	
Spain	105,100	25,990	497,200	665,100	3,250	5,750	706,430	504,070		
Italy	4,019,200	1,343,080	1,828,450	1,124,880	562,770	708,920	1,244,440	2,663,690	1,158,8:	2,263,700
Roumania										1,818,200
Turkey	9,342,000	3,785,000	3,731,600	8,337,000	3,145,000	8,939,000	5,329,850	3,469,820	5,464,000	1,783,400
Egypt							549,080	461,180		826,400
East Indies								183,760		2,071,300
Australia									1,393,600	3,899,500
United States, Atlantic ports	5,459,300	1,120,600	3,600,570	3,591,300	29,260	085,650	1,015,990	31,794,620	72,542,170	63,887,590
United States, Pacific ports	532,200	180,500	656,700	3,209,000	25,900	127,300	176,830	885,500	6,567,000	7,492,900
English Possessions in North America								611,650		506,400
Chili	913,000	474,000	643,000	2,502,000	23,500	104,600	3,763,360	1,015,000	1,287,700	2,126,600
Algeria	2,134,000	3,822,000	6,148,000	4,825,000	2,398,000	4,495,000	97,540	797,380	2,538,980	5,529,490
Other countries	7,181,510	1,581,960	5,622,610	5,996,500	705,400	1,242,260			2,155,700	730,700
Total	71,719,400	25,065,400	34,057,900	50,644,350	17,065,730	27,827,650	20,519,500	80,928,700	133,615,960	117,947,400

7.—Statement showing the quantities of rye imported into France, and the countries and colonies from which imported, during each of the years specified below.

Countries.	1871.	1872.	1873.	1874.	1875.	1876.	1877.	1878.	1879.	1880.
	Bushels.	Bushels.	Bushels.	Bushels.	Bushels.	Bushels.	Bushels.	Bushels.	Bushels.	Bushels.
Russia:										
White Sea								33,090	565,960	100,000
Black Sea								177,310	1,096,800	548,800
Denmark										98,690
Germany										
Belgium	61,100	5,400	32,700	65,900	18,700	19,470		8,180	536,320	179,090
Austria							37,240	283,190	497,900	115,040
England							47,300	2,250	3,770	
Spain				167,500	4,850	40,600	114,480			
Turkey	60,900	22,400	40,400	39,540	1,920		28,500	72,480	290,500	86,570
United States	37,400	930	7,240			4,970			236,860	296,200
Other countries	76,120	28,360	44,680	228,520	34,210	10,040	47,110	56,080	86,200	29,740
Total	235,520	55,090	125,020	501,460	59,680	75,080	274,630	634,060	3,256,040	1,544,130

Statement showing the value of rye imported into France, and the countries and colonies from which imported, during each of the years specified below.

Countries.	1871.	1872.	1873.	1874.	1875.	1876.	1877.	1878.	1879.	1880.
Russia:										
White Sea								$28,080	$568,700	$204,900
Black Sea								147,800	1,104,000	591,900
Denmark										106,400
Germany										
Belgium	$65,820	$5,190	$32,110	$66,220	$15,780	$17,100		10,830	542,060	207,280
Austria							$35,830	238,520	478,300	129,250
England							47,460	2,780	6,080	
Spain				108,300	4,110	35,680	110,100			
Turkey	65,640	21,450	30,570	39,860	1,630		27,160	60,400	261,800	93,370
United States	40,320	800	7,100			4,300			230,100	319,500
Other countries	85,490	27,450	47,010	232,840	32,400	19,460	45,560	47,760	91,700	37,900
Total	257,270	54,080	125,790	507,210	53,920	76,870	266,310	536,170	3,288,740	1,600,480

8.—Statement showing the quantities of maize imported into France, and the countries and colonies from which imported, during each of the years specified below.

Countries	1871	1872	1873	1874	1875	1876	1877	1878	1879	1880
	Bushels.	Bushels.	Bushels.	Bushels.	Bushels.	Bushels.	Bushels.	Bushels.	Bushels.	Bushels.
Russia:										
White Sea							416,500			559,500
Black Sea	124,700	41,680	994,000	315,400	88,060	748,600	272,200	2,035,500	1,390,000	5,620
Belgium	61,720	114,500	192,000	216,100	673,900	476,600	208,840	54,010	161,100	154,500
Italy								229,740	212,290	631,700
Roumania	565,900	375,500	1,331,000	377,000	146,300	3,215,000	2,533,000	3,238,000	4,415,200	405,200
Turkey										
Egypt							87,100			
United States	240,900	188,900	406,500	618,000	28,540	347,000	1,898,000	3,010,000	3,210,000	11,463,000
Argentine Republic	41,250	41,450	35,050	30,760	66,450	58,440		181,500	469,700	368,700
Other countries	123,000	160,610	269,500	196,200	53,800	214,000	136,850	153,250	213,880	177,850
Total	1,157,470	922,650	3,228,080	1,753,460	1,057,950	5,057,640	5,554,930	8,902,000	10,078,170	13,766,070

Statement showing the value of maize imported into France, and the countries and colonies from which imported, during each of the years specified below.

Countries	1871	1872	1873	1874	1875	1876	1877	1878	1879	1880
Russia:										
White Sea							$306,300			$438,900
Black Sea	$140,400	$38,830	$926,000	$309,200	$90,720	$568,900	200,200	$1,297,000	$1,095,000	4,430
Belgium	69,600	106,600	178,700	211,800	611,200	362,300	2,300	38,020	125,400	140,460
Italy							160,520	170,310	189,800	495,600
Roumania	638,300	349,700	1,240,000	369,800	132,800	2,443,000	1,862,000	2,222,000	2,518,000	317,800
Turkey										
Egypt							64,000			
United States	271,600	178,000	378,700	606,000	25,890	263,800	1,396,000	2,066,000	3,463,000	8,991,000
Argentine Republic								124,600	368,400	289,200
Other countries	200,080	198,360	290,750	228,390	123,710	219,740	101,570	105,600	168,950	140,970
Total	1,319,080	869,490	3,014,150	1,725,190	974,320	3,857,740	4,092,890	6,123,530	7,929,610	10,818,360

CEREAL CROPS OF GERMANY.

REPORT BY VICE-CONSUL-GENERAL ZIMMERMAN, OF BERLIN, ON THE CEREAL CROPS OF GERMANY. AND ON THE IMPORTS AND EXPORTS OF CEREALS.

In compliance with circular instructions of the Department, dated May 31, 1882, I endeavored to gather all the information called for therein; but I regret to have to report that crop statistics were not kept in Germany previous to the year 1878. Up to that time some of the states of the German Empire compiled, to a greater or lesser extent, statistical information on the subject from quite different points of view, and for different years; other states published no statistics at all. Under such circumstances it was impossible to compare and collect satisfactory crop statistics for those years.

On the 8th of November, 1877, however, the German Federal Council by a resolution provided for the collection of uniform crop statistics throughout the German Empire, to commence with the year 1878.

As to the countries to which wheat, rye, and maize were exported, or from which they were imported, no statistics were kept at an earlier period than the year 1878, and even from and after that time the countries are not uniformly given.

Thus in 1878 and 1879, instead of showing, as in 1880 and 1881, the exports to and imports from the United States and England and some other countries, only general statements of said exports and imports through Baltic and North Sea ports appear.

Concerning the value of goods imported and exported, I have to state that the figures submitted represent but estimates of value, as the German duties are collected by weight. For 1880 and 1881 I have been enabled to report the values of imported and exported cereals also by countries.

F. C. ZIMMERMAN,
Vice-Consul-General.

UNITED STATES CONSULATE-GENERAL,
Vienna, August 21, 1882.

Table showing the area under each cereal crop and the quantities and yield of each cereal for the years 1878 to 1881, inclusive.

Cereals.	1878.		1879.	
	Acres.	Bushels.	Acres.	Bushels.
Wheat	4,534,292	91,251,510	4,494,502	82,060,225
German wheat (Spelt)	966,752	15,642,410	967,328	16,109,080
One-grained wheat	20,992	200,365	20,352	244,860
Rye	14,837,022	276,786,680	14,648,058	222,497,400
Barley	4,051,127	198,960,442	4,013,743	94,628,468
Oats	9,357,290	247,776,560	9,252,851	293,780,481
Maize	52,040	(*)	52,680	579,320

Cereals.	1880.		1881.	
	Acres.	Bushels.	Acres.	Bushels.
Wheat	4,483,617	83,084,730	4,543,517	72,069,865
German wheat (Spelt)	1,054,449	17,126,900	944,842	15,715,805
One-grained wheat	17,089	217,805	17,590	213,850
Rye	14,624,049	198,101,000	14,783,712	217,936,160
Barley	4,011,277	98,698,382	3,083,195	95,503,360
Oats	9,245,832	291,740,832	8,361,587	259,435,141
Maize	43,565	427,320	(†)	

* Not published.　　　　† Statistics no longer collected.

*Quantities and value of exported.**

Years.	Wheat.		Rye.		Maize.	
	Bushels.	Dollars.	Bushels.	Dollars.	Bushels.	Dollars.
	Thousands.	*Thousands.*	*Thousands.*	*Thousands.*	*Thousands.*	*Thousands.*
1872	14,210	23,205	3,180	3,046	41	35
1873	11,970	20,990	6,360	6,810	119.2	107
1874	13,755	22,419	6,800	7,282	82.8	86
1875	19,950	28,560	6,240	5,926	848	804
1876	12,580	20,325	4,000	4,046	776	737
1877	25,725	38,556	7,040	7,092	848	756
1878	27,475	37,366	7,840	6,907	828	687
1879	21,175	30,226	5,840	5,188	620	440
1880	6,235	9,621	1,083	1,223	54.3	44
1881	8,764	13,094	2,387	2,879	23.2	10

Countries to, and seas, &c., through which exported.

IN 1878.

Whither.	Wheat.	Rye.	Maize.
	Bushels.	*Bushels.*	*Bushels.*
Denmark	13,843	10,006	880
Baltic Sea	19,049	5,170,986	38,808
Russia	21,769	17,058	5,030
Austria-Hungary	1,144,068	1,556,456	215,302
Switzerland	5,878,605	79,856	425,674
France	690,377	15,170	2,824
Belgium	427,635	30,786	400
Netherlands	276,246	54,596	1,152
North Sea	111,981	7,360	
Bremen	106,421	135,996	15,856
Hamburg	1,216,886	577,650	136,374
Ports of Prussia (not included in the Zollverein)	329,488	199,402	80
Oldenburg		606	480

IN 1880.

Whither.	Wheat.		Rye.		Maize.	
	Bushels.	Dollars.	Bushels.	Dollars.	Bushels.	Dollars.
	Thousands.	*Thousands.*	*Thousands.*	*Thousands.*	*Thousands.*	*Thousands.*
Bremen			28	32		
Hamburg-Altona	625	1,099	313	359		
Denmark	300	759	42	47		
Norway	114	172	465	533		
Sweden	106	160	77	88		
Russia	138	209				
Austria-Hungary	720	109	554	635		
Switzerland	2,389	3,617			213	177
France	589	894				
Belgium	1,217	1,846	185	212		
Netherlands	337	461	375	461	347	242
Great Britain	2,591	3,927				

IN 1881.

	Wheat.		Rye.		Maize.	
	Bushels.	Dollars.	Bushels.	Dollars.	Bushels.	Dollars.
Bremen			24	25		
Hamburg-Altona	472	654	343	362	3.2	2.28
Denmark	1,460	2,027	177	187		
Norway	205	285	1,040	1,094		
Russia					13	9
Sweden	998	1,386	367	387		
Austria-Hungary	403	559	214	225	60	43
Switzerland	1,537	2,160			143	102
Belgium	539	748	34	36		
France					2.3	1
Netherlands	628	872	62	65		
Great Britain	2,627	3,649	116	122		

* Where thousands are at the heads of columns in the following tables it would seem to imply that 000's are omitted. The tables are given substantially as made up by the German authorities.

Quantities and value of imported.

Years.	Wheat.		Rye.		Maize.	
	Bushels.	Dollars.	Bushels.	Dollars.	Bushels.	Dollars.
	Thousands.	*Thousands.*	*Thousands.*	*Thousands.*	*Thousands.*	*Thousands.*
1872	10, 710	17, 493	22, 000	21, 205	720	616
1873	12. 810	22, 491	31, 200	33, 415	1, 160	1, 035
1874	14, 280	23, 276	38, 000	40, 698	2, 260	2, 177
1875	18. 465	24, 990	28, 000	26, 656	4, 520	4, 284
1876	23, 975	35, 938	44, 000	44, 744	7, 860	7, 473
1877	32, 900	49, 000	47, 600	48, 076	7, 120	6, 354
1878	37, 100	50, 218	37, 800	33, 796	4, 680	3, 808
1879	31, 725	45, 690	58, 800	52. 360	8, 000	5, 712
1880	7, 964	12, 287	35, 582	31, 719	13, 625	10, 900
1881	22, 627	32, 368	24, 610	26, 180	18, 037	12, 852

Countries from, and seas, &c., through which imported.

IN 1878.

Whence.	Wheat.	Rye.	Maize.
	Bushels.	*Bushels.*	*Bushels.*
Denmark	15, 453	35, 456	4, 782
Baltic Sea	745, 092	5, 831, 894	35, 578
Russia	13, 982, 689	13, 443, 902	....
Austria-Hungary	15, 121, 751	3, 488, 562	1, 681, 852
Switzerland	619, 041	22, 526	19, 896
France	55, 344	1, 284, 690	5, 984
Belgium	1, 771, 264	1, 193, 126	92, 948
Netherlands	5, 445, 158	6, 365, 330	473, 702
North Sea	99, 678	1, 105, 228	58, 282
Bremen	300, 636	2, 579, 640	1, 193, 334
Hamburg	339, 024	1, 407, 234	863, 918
Ports of Prussia (not included in the Zollverein)	132, 533	1, 091, 998	229, 454
Oldenburg	1, 855	200, 976	17, 484

IN 1879.

Denmark	25, 198	46, 520	792
Baltic Sea	794, 628	19, 537, 458	31, 142
Russia	8, 731, 330	11, 726, 730	34
Austria-Hungary	12, 851, 908	3, 555. 922	2, 661, 456
Switzerland	278, 190	9, 720	9, 818
France	44, 042	683, 058	8, 034
Belgium	1, 862, 470	1, 752, 426	133, 668
Netherlands	7, 682, 551	11, 278, 996	687, 368
North Sea	76, 095	1, 931, 664	39, 280
Bremen	351, 601	4, 543, 680	1, 770, 234
Hamburg	450, 466	1, 912, 302	2, 538, 844
Ports of Prussia (not included in the Zollverein)	107, 511	1, 978, 878	280, 990
Oldenburg	3, 336	226, 068	7, 956

Whence.	Wheat.		Rye.		Maize.	
	Bushels.	Dollars.	Bushels.	Dollars.	Bushels.	Dollars.
	Thousands.	*Thousands.*	*Thousands.*	*Thousands.*	*Thousands.*	*Thousands.*
Bremen	209	285	1,557	157	2,278	1,599
Hamburg-Altona	488	668	905	916	4,185	590
Denmark	103	140	668	670	225	158
Sweden			55	55		
Russia	5,924	7,830	15,786	1,990	372	261
Austria-Hungary	4,486	6,140	2,577	2,618	841	590
France			2,526	2,546		
Belgium	596	816	1,214	1,228	289	202
Netherlands	338	461	702	706	347	242
Roumania	545	747	39	39	601	421
Bulgaria.			11	10		
Turkey					211	148
Egypt	14	19				
British India	16	21				
North America	14	17	27	27	650	456
United States	3,822	5,236	297	299	4,042	2,832
Ports of South America	6	8	9	8	44	30

IN 1881.

Bremen	237	329	1,634	1,727	3,422	2,437
Hamburg	579	803	808	853	5,254	3,743
Denmark			423	447		
Russia	11,188	15,539	12,359	13,069	1,059	754
Austria-Hungary	4,479	6,221	2,217	2,344	1,046	745
France			3,693	3,905		
Belgium	1,031	1,431	2,041	2,159	1,034	714
Netherlands	551	738	856	906	648	461
Roumania	487	076			1,705	1,214
United States	4,076	5,661	206	218	3,250	2,322
Other countries	665	923	373	394	609	434

CEREAL AND CROP REPORTS IN HOLLAND.

REPORT BY CONSUL ECKSTEIN, OF AMSTERDAM.

Reports on the results of the harvest of any year are not required to be sent in to the government from the various districts before January of each succeeding year, and then it takes the government from a year to eighteen months more before it finally publishes the agricultural statistics for such years. It is only very recently that those covering the year 1880 made their appearance, nor will any sort of agricultural report for 1882 be likely to be forthcoming before late in the year 1884. And then again it should be stated that the form in which they are generally prepared in this country cannot be at all compared with that in which our own national and State bureaus of statistics publish them, being neither as complete nor as comprehensive, and when brought out so late they have lost nearly all value for any practical purposes.

This year, for the first time, the government requested or ordered a kind of provisional report regarding the state of the growing crops to be made at an earlier day than usual by the different districts or provinces.

D. ECKSTEIN,
Consul.

UNITED STATES CONSULATE,
Amsterdam, October 11, 1882.

CEREALS IN BELGIUM.

REPORT BY CONSUL STEUART, OF ANTWERP.

Referring to circular from the Department of State, dated 31st May last, I have now the honor to hand the accompanying tables, giving the information asked for in the third and fourth questions of the circular, viz:

Table No. 1 gives the quantities and values of the total importations and exportations of wheat, rye, and corn into and from Belgium for the ten years from 1871 to 1880, inclusive.

Table No. 2 gives the quantities of wheat, rye, and corn imported into Belgium for the same period of time according to the countries from which they came.

Table No. 3 gives the quantities of wheat, rye, and corn exported from Belgium and the countries to which exported during the years mentioned.

The quantities are given in bushels and the value in dollars.

Corn, oats, and buckwheat are always given together in the official returns, so that I could not separate them.

In regard to questions 1 and 2 in the circular, I addressed myself to the minister of the interior for the desired information, but in his reply, dated 21st July, he tells me that the government has no data upon the quantity of land cultivated in Belgium since a report made in 1866, but that new agricultural statistics have been collected to the end of 1880, and that so soon as they are in order for use I should be notified of the result.

JOHN H. STEUART,
Consul.

UNITED STATES CONSULATE,
Antwerp, August 2, 1882.

1.—Table showing the exportations of wheat, rye, and corn from Belgium, and the countries to which exported, for the ten years from 1871 to 1880, inclusive.

Countries.	Cereals.	1871. Bushels.	1872. Bushels.	1873. Bushels.	1874. Bushels.	1875. Bushels.	1876. Bushels.	1877. Bushels.	1878. Bushels.	1870. Bushels.	1889. Bushels.
England, by sea	Wheat	1,833	9,166	440	154,890	35,713	6,856	43,706	11,660	55,403	
	Rye				390		783			21,803	73
	Corn, oats, and buckwheat				8,232		943		19,446		
France, by land	Wheat	74,603	1,366,003	2,435	1,574,833	82,382	1,197,570	1,201,310	2,479,620	4,213,293	2,480,783
	Rye	35,420	725,266	992,493	43,135	444,363	8,759	35,632	232,178	314,128	72,875
	Corn, oats, and buckwheat	3,260	5,814	22,580	295,978	9,350	412,028	430,178	1,217,542	1,299,257	856,625
Germany, by land and sea	Wheat	163,389	280,085	156,357	1,399,456	277,946	1,804,146	991,980	1,749,073	2,707,503	2,263,590
	Rye		176,366	1,224,080	1,143,017	676,170	1,708,928	2,369,446	2,746,460	4,918,375	2,152,345
	Corn, oats, and buckwheat		534,560	1,110,371	229,310	852,183	742,421	1,103,575	1,691,828	1,170,439	851,085
Holland, by land and sea	Wheat	36,457	184,132	134,671	1,108,433	252,567	1,975,490	961,693	659,890	1,090,740	1,584,623
	Rye	14,923	314,013	910,946	997,228	1,253,706	1,277,060	1,126,439	905,653	903,532	923,292
	Corn, oats, and buckwheat	32,646	1,090,357	1,338,228	72,757	1,200,296	104,107	247,107	302,185	306,192	438,900
Luxemburg, by land	Wheat	11,432	27,264	55,745	37,840	70,635	25,586	144,173	205,186	330,696	173,396
	Rye	22,806	43,046	53,973	121,707	39,416	57,042	118,839	119,785	277,671	174,075
	Corn, oats, and buckwheat	116,639	69,614	104,940	14,573	29,228	14,614	22,432	52,564	16,696	19,446
Switzerland, by land	Wheat	18,857	33,589	7,071	480,553	1,335	771,540	185,460	176,585	527,230	1,091,125
	Rye			117,886		156,640		390	6,325	101,121	101,121
	Corn, oats, and buckwheat									140,446	46,675
Spain, by sea	Wheat				2,475		37,871	68,121	95,464	4,475	144,760
	Rye			7,267	5,185					707	
	Corn, oats, and buckwheat								10,670		4,714

2.—*Table showing the importations into Belgium of wheat, rye, and corn, and the countries from which received, for the ten years from 1871 to 1880, inclusive.*

Countries.	Cereals.	1871.	1872.	1873.	1874.	1875.	1876.	1877.	1878.	1879.	1880.
		Bushels.	Bushels.	Bushels.	Bushels.	Bushels.	Bushels.	Bushels.	Bushels.	Bushels.	Bushels.
Austria, by sea	Wheat	175,486	30					269,096	68,750		
	Rye	5,971						20,155			
	Corn, oats, and buckwheat							68,157			
Chili, by sea	Wheat	19,053	140,643	3,850	250,506	392	30,800		70,714		
	Rye										
	Corn, oats, and buckwheat			261,880						58,116	
Denmark, by sea	Wheat	1,642,556	791,120	542,776	397,576	393,250	260,333	129,213	343,760	44,440	12,833
	Rye	195,800	15,321	23,178	8,092	11,117	29,621				
	Corn, oats, and buckwheat	3,234			117,071					106,659	33,550
England, by sea	Wheat	1,806,090	440,476	1,203,840	348,700	95,626	1,134,576	728,796	485,503	249,443	899,770
	Rye	31,389	1,492	4,557	314	6,757			16,064	34,728	98,685
	Corn, oats, and buckwheat	19,132	4,282	33,982	2,553	7,542	33,353	15,439	27,185	33,335	108,742
English India, by sea	Wheat						117,180	331,283			203,683
	Rye										
	Corn, oats, and buckwheat										23,285
English possessions in America, by sea	Wheat	580					88,000	11,442		73,700	2,073
	Rye										
	Corn, oats, and buckwheat										131,214
Egypt, by sea	Wheat			316,343	66,073		304,700	176,370		181,500	699,160
	Rye									30,446	254,257
	Corn, oats, and buckwheat									264,510	311,353
France, by land and water	Wheat	253,476	1,262,946	934,303	856,790	2,061,163	653,906	1,148,326	100,320	128,810	131,156
	Rye	1,224,850	1,854,992	1,695,414	834,271	1,630,632	1,448,700	1,018,757	391,588	194,417	491,371
	Corn, oats, and buckwheat	100,296	32,121	707,142	590,975	288,396	185,271	193,651	157,246	170,264	268,007
Germany, by land and sea	Wheat	5,096,666	1,300,406	1,407,230	2,084,866	2,110,240	2,144,266	3,339,410	4,603,410	2,760,977	1,867,526
	Rye	1,769,246	44,235	199,371	199,371	23,275	96,849	66,589	228,132	443,714	440,391
	Corn, oats, and buckwheat	465,025	4,714	171,875	338,407	158,685	270,875	272,403	712,210	764,421	513,082
Holland, by land	Wheat	404,383	614,313	892,760	875,013	922,056	1,171,820	732,636	893,750	916,960	1,056,073
	Rye	415,367	43,942	185,350	117,385	68,328	68,632	27,696		97,175	79,475
	Corn, oats, and buckwheat	577,185	232,257	233,290	309,457	380,482	613,721	556,364	433,989	228,367	297,942
Italy, by sea	Wheat	2,126					217,800	184,920			
	Rye										
	Corn, oats, and buckwheat						1,767				
Luxemburg, by land	Wheat	341,440	237,746	204,820	21,890	17,600	18,778	58,263	47,142		
	Rye	52,132	11,707	2,082	4,596	64,350	38,940		37,033		
	Corn, oats, and buckwheat	8,878		104,578	104,085	124,928	311		2,062		
Portugal, by sea	Wheat			128,626	47,666		66,707	21,921	49,971	71,617	66,982
	Rye				2,300						
	Corn, oats, and buckwheat							29,480	1,571		
Russia, by sea	Wheat	1,138,390	2,034,428	1,991,293	2,543,423	2,805,110	3,680,216	1,872,090	3,566,676	4,455,000	2,628,193
	Rye	836,196	644,678	759,214	2,014,610	1,688,343	3,008,285	2,459,560	4,847,060	3,132,045	1,854,900
	Corn, oats, and buckwheat	1,059,692	311,800	739,750	1,612,757	1,056,078	2,327,757	2,253,939	3,450,857	3,791,857	2,810,225

Origin	Kind									
Rio de la Plata, by sea	Wheat	1,100		17,343		60,666			177,833		
Spain, by sea	Wheat	6,196		5,028	51,582	28,966	130,467	100,943	55,432	102,300	
	Rye			348,076	62,603				16,290		120,450
	Corn, oats, and buckwheat		18,646	982	5,735		233	134,592	2,575		
Sweden and Norway, by sea	Wheat	336,160	95,626	108,130	18,186	99,230	9,780	97,826	60,940		64,240
	Rye	26,714	471			4,439				4,094	
	Corn, oats, and buckwheat	498,535	1,021	85,878	410,928	641,103	241,646	451,785	791,017		610,535
Turkey, by sea	Wheat	657,103	134,530		168,410	462,146	1,108,066	471,863	137,814	542,170	216,086
	Rye	258,223	198,157	91,653	142,567	172,071	703,528	758,214	171,560	627,150	130,800
	Corn, oats, and buckwheat			44,235		58,321	161,346	184,564	80,653		
United States, by sea	Wheat	1,569,876	313,023	2,945,800	5,565,366	2,007,023	3,577,090	2,672,780	6,903,380	12,962,860	14,837,276
	Rye	82,617	50,285	240,507	226,757	34,335	58,062	1,013,689	766,025	2,173,227	828,374
	Corn, oats, and buckwheat	9,821		90,178	27,264	109,725		413,696	1,336,185	1,621,910	3,374,800
Others, by land and sea	Wheat	1,063		27,903	74,935	1,101	8,543	22,766	235	123,015	424,072
	Rye							10,607			50,857
	Corn, oats, and buckwheat	3,732	12,375			38,502		25,810			3,732

3.—*Table showing the quantities and value of wheat, rye, and corn imported into Belgium for the ten years from 1871 to 1880, inclusive.*

Products.	1871.	1872.	1873.	1874.	1875.	1876.	1877.	1878.	1879.	1880.
Wheat:										
Quantity .... bushels..	13,970,550	8,008,183	11,384,780	13,418,350	10,971,070	16,639,668	12,132,230	17,014,176	22,991,870	23,241,863
Value	$26,479,022	$13,913,899	$20,879,343	$23,313,706	$15,015,339	$24,530,115	$20,440,347	$25,978,185	$32,644,169	$33,486,872
Rye:										
Quantity .... bushels..	4,820,867	2,877,403	3,978,189	3,556,104	3,652,628	4,392,850	5,321,332	6,661,403	8,022,907	4,130,882
Value	$6,159,265	$2,827,992	$4,496,332	$4,368,725	$3,576,270	$4,317,374	$6,240,347	$6,546,911	$8,471,710	$4,668,919
Corn, oats, and buckwheat:										
Quantity .... bushels..	2,869,350	341,667	2,280,775	3,774,453	2,404,992	4,468,353	4,296,935	6,924,430	7,702,714	8,502,307
Value	$3,243,030	$385,551	$2,333,011	$4,630,872	$2,718,146	$5,072,779	$4,634,565	$6,815,250	$7,275,655	$8,385,521

Table showing the quantities and value of wheat, rye, and corn exported from Belgium for the ten years from 1871 to 1880, inclusive.

Products.	1871.	1872.	1873.	1874.	1875.	1876.	1877.	1878.	1879.	1880.
Wheat:										
Quantity .... bushels..	394,020	1,268,263	2,295,820	4,755,940	2,606,010	6,014,360	3,528,323	5,300,020	8,924,886	8,594,666
Value	$746,911	$2,203,474	$6,073,359	$8,263,320	$3,567,374	$8,846,409	$5,944,584	$8,081,081	$12,687,258	$13,122,779
Rye:										
Quantity .... bushels..	132,585	1,691,014	2,588,653	2,307,957	2,091,080	3,052,775	3,650,389	4,001,328	6,541,307	3,371,303
Value	$194,980	$1,661,989	$2,923,675	$1,835,328	$2,055,019	$3,000,386	$4,126,675	$3,932,432	$6,428,764	$4,810,231
Corn, oats, and buckwheat:										
Quantity .... bushels..	307,860	1,791,075	361,625	627,078	684,867	1,312,025	1,873,378	2,779,071	2,936,800	2,367,907
Value	$346,911	$1,496,332	$373,165	$770,463	$774,131	$1,482,818	$2,025,289	$2,731,274	$2,742,084	$2,827,220

CEREALS OF THE UNITED KINGDOM.

REPORT BY CONSUL-GENERAL MERRITT, OF LONDON.

In response to the circular of the Department of State of the 31st of May, 1882, requesting statistical information as to the cereal productions of Great Britain and the amounts of the imports and exports of grains for the last ten years, I have the honor to submit herewith my report. For its preparation I have mainly relied upon the very full and accurate statistical tables published by the government, but when, as in certain instances, the government returns did not contain the desired information, recourse has been had to the best unofficial authorities with a view of making the report as complete as possible. Where the tables are capable of fuller explanation, a few comments have been added, calling attention to the more important facts elicited by the statistics, especially as bearing upon the interests of American commerce and agriculture.

The circular calls for information for each of the last ten years (1872, 1881) upon the following points:

I.—The area under each cereal crop for the year specified.

Description of crops.	1872.	1873.	1874.	1875.	1876.
	Acres.	*Acres.*	*Acres.*	*Acres.*	*Acres.*
Cultivated area......................	31,003,137	31,102,620	31,266,919	31,416,350	31,551,612
CORN CROPS.					
Wheat..................................	3,598,957	3,102,620	3,630,300	3,342,481	2,995,957
Barley or bere..........................	2,316,332	2,335,913	2,287,987	2,509,701	2,533,109
Oats....................................	2,705,837	2,676,227	2,596,384	2,684,009	2,798,430
Rye.....................................	66,875	51,634	47,228	54,903	56,210
Beans...................................	524,005	586,561	559,044	564,181	517,556
Peas....................................	361,545	318,213	310,547	316,375	293,407
Total..................................	9,573,551	9,458,928	9,431,490	9,451,650	9,194,669

Description of crops.	1877.	1878.	1879.	1880.	1881.
	Acres.	*Acres.*	*Acres.*	*Acres.*	*Acres.*
Cultivated area...........................	31,711,413	31,854,532	31,975,784	32,101,909	32,211,512
CORN CROPS.					
Wheat..................................	3,188,540	3,218,417	2,890,244	2,909,438	2,805,809
Barley or bere..........................	2,417,588	2,469,652	2,667,176	2,467,441	2,442,334
Oats....................................	2,754,179	2,698,907	2,656,628	2,796,905	2,801,275
Rye.....................................	60,146	60,117	49,127	40,781	41,567
Beans...................................	497,879	437,936	444,328	426,667	440,201
Peas....................................	311,797	282,617	277,831	234,470	216,790
Total..................................	9,210,129	9,167,646	8,985,234	8,875,702	8,847,976

An advance abstract of the agricultural statistics of this year (1882) shows the wheat acreage to be 3,003,915; oats, 2,833,815; and barley, 2,255,139; a gain of acreage in wheat of 7.1 per cent. and a loss in oats of 2.3 per cent., and a loss in barley of 7.7 per cent., as compared with the returns of last year.

This increase in wheat was a surprise, as the last seven bad years in

English agriculture have fallen most heavily upon the wheat-growers A leading writer, in commenting upon these statistics recently, said:

It is a question whether an increased area under wheat is not a greater cause for alarm than a slight decrease. The vast and almost exhaustless prairie lands of the Middle, Western, and Northwestern States and Territories of the great American continent are being brought into cultivation, and the stored-up fertility of these lands has been such, that, up to the present time, and probably for many years to come, enormous crops have been grown at a cost that to us in this country seems absolutely incredible. India, also, with her vast lands, is now fast flooding the European markets at prices that barely exceed the cost of raising the crop in this country.

Speaking of raising wheat on the poorer English lands, he says:

It is to be feared that the increase under wheat this year means that many of these unprofitable lands—driven out of cultivation by bad seasons—have once again been put under wheat. If this is the case they will be in the future a source of vexation to us. In very good years they will but barely pay their cost of working, while in bad seasons they will be a constant source of anxiety and loss.

The reduction in the barley average is attributed to the great reduction in prices which Mr. Gladstone's rearrangement of the malt tax has brought about. The effect of foreign competition and bad seasons has been to reduce the wheat average in twelve years about 25 per cent., the other cereals with some slight variations remaining the same from year to year. In wheat the highest point was reached in 1869 with 3,981,989 acres under cultivation, and the lowest in 1881, with 2,967,059.

II.—*The quantities and yield of each cereal for each year.*

WHEAT.

	Bushels.
1872	88,320,000
1873	91,750,000
1874	118,823,000
1875	80,822,000
1876	84,248,000
1877	73,062,000
1878	101,460,000
1879	55,008,000
1880	79,590,000
1881	77,954,000

BARLEY.

Average acreage	2,680,378
Average yield per acre ....bushels..	36
Average production ....do.....	96,493,608

OATS.

Average acreage	4,196,226
Average yield per acre ....bushels..	48
Average production ....do.....	201,418,848

RYE.

Average acreage	61,880
Average yield per acre ....bushels..	32
Average production ....do.....	1,980,160

The government statisticians in Great Britain make no effort to collect the total amount of grain produced, except as the returns of sales show the probable quantities. I have, therefore, in the tables of wheat and the averages given for barley, oats, and rye, followed the best unofficial statistics obtainable. The prominent feature of these returns is the larger yield per acre as compared with corresponding returns in American agriculture, and they bear testimony to the high cultivation of the land, and the skill and labor of the English farmer under what has been of late years most discouraging circumstances.

The standard average of wheat, for example, is 29½ bushels per acre, while in the United States, according to late official figures, the yield per acre is only 12.4 bushels. I call particular attention to this point, as furnishing a contrast which may hereafter be of value to our American farmers. With a wheat acreage twelve times greater than Great Britain, the United States does not produce six times as much wheat.

III.—*The quantities and value of wheat, rye, and maize exported, and the countries and colonies to which exported, whether by sea or land, for each year.*

EXPORTS OF BREADSTUFFS.

Year.	Value.	Year.	Value.
1872	$3,110,764	1877	$2,307,764
1873	5,383,983	1878	3,324,914
1874	3,199,422	1879	3,409,421
1875	1,930,443	1880	3,508,897
1876	3,018,198	1881	3,712,015

Great Britain being pre-eminently an exporting country in manufactures and importing in cereals, the very small exports of breadstuffs make unnecessary a more detailed statement as to quantities and destinations.

Maize is not raised here. Rye is of so little importance that its acreage is only ½ per cent. of the land under cereal cultivation.

The average yield of wheat of about 80,000,000 bushels is all consumed, and with a population of over 37,000,000 it requires in addition about 110,000,000 bushels to supply home needs.

These facts will appear more clearly by a comparison of the exports of breadstuffs with the imports, as given below.

V.— *The quantities and value of wheat, rye, and maize imported, and the countries and colonies from which imported for each year.*

[Stated in cwts. according to present system of entry.]

WHEAT.

Countries.	1872.	1873.	1874.	1875.	1876.	1877.	1878.	1879.	1880.	1881.
	Cwts.	Cwts.	Cwts.	Cwts.	Cwts.	Cwts.	Cwts.	Cwts.	Cwts.	Cwts.
Russia:										
Northern ports	2,080,175	1,816,787	709,576	1,688,035	1,977,346	6,960,764	4,125,785	3,044,502	244,216	426,852
Southern ports	15,775,463	7,778,862	5,016,085	8,317,280	6,803,282	3,807,472	4,895,894	4,960,089	2,636,108	3,619,797
Sweden	44,566	34,058	23,981	99,590	58,411	33,003	16,363	20,688	5,086	829
Denmark	428,654	301,758	188,351	493,019	263,205	73,812	139,987	58,580	30,641	
Germany	3,891,062	2,155,173	3,063,032	5,612,546	2,324,148	5,455,144	5,117,995	3,613,878	1,599,143	1,361,402
France	2,844,811	1,170,262	309,297	1,297,843	292,050	1,492,768	11,196	17,291	1,446	6,693
Spain	551,991	671,348	179,181	148,761	243,744	463,416	55,896	3,694	31	
Austrian territories	55,186	11,530	2,337	18,544	4,556	42,858	11,048	19,745	11,502	10,412
Roumania	266,163	124,540	53,408	347,843	379,079	229,808	65,075	158,854	126,629	214,855
Turkey	559,008	295,207	567,427	957,965	862,884	1,022,850	143,301	11,500	4,005	29,277
Egypt	2,340,227	1,261,230	293,880	2,107,859	2,223,238	2,447,681	217,003	2,055,697	1,601,281	1,070,710
British North America	1,734,982	3,761,863	3,811,575	3,622,675	2,453,183	2,951,891	2,620,820	4,781,736	3,887,582	2,875,606
United States:										
Atlantic ports	7,328,054	12,693,151	18,063,902	14,935,326	12,737,096	12,522,039	24,468,189	29,107,312	29,634,820	24,820,246
Pacific ports	1,391,886	7,103,263	5,026,189	8,587,981	6,585,958	8,864,941	4,592,620	6,934,583	6,555,994	11,263,242
Chili	1,436,351	1,574,744	1,926,456	884,235	982,379	736,011	50,573	1,400,394	1,348,206	1,094,261
British India	156,665	740,934	1,073,940	1,334,366	3,287,236	6,104,985	1,820,881	887,006	3,229,050	7,334,616
Australasia	500,589	1,801,363	907,453	1,156,843	2,605,540	425,697	1,453,814	2,727,005	4,246,376	2,968,730
Other countries	741,873	567,005	320,508	260,388	401,813	574,080	68,034	262,641	99,858	50,405
Total	42,127,726	43,863,098	41,527,638	51,876,517	44,454,657	54,269,800	49,906,484	59,591,795	55,261,924	57,147,933

[Total of grain and flour in equivalent weight of grain (1 cwt. of wheat flour) = 1½ cwt. of wheat in grain).]

Countries.	1872.	1873.	1874.	1875.	1876.	1877.	1878.	1879.	1880.	1881.
Russia:										
Northern ports	2,080,939	1,817,005	710,002	1,688,141	1,977,546	7,055,850	4,133,198	3,045,514	244,463	426,948
Southern ports	15,858,038	7,876,392	6,098,974	8,460,706	6,934,742	3,948,067	5,016,953	5,071,971	2,719,296	3,673,024
Sweden	44,582	34,058	24,077	100,052	58,420	36,453	16,707	22,082	5,086	
Denmark	611,283	475,354	455,394	831,850	852,030	670,083	638,072	554,893	418,911	368,010
Germany	5,183,601	3,019,406	4,012,066	6,613,544	3,487,672	7,004,380	6,541,560	4,757,794	2,821,164	3,096,326
France	4,553,781	3,259,619	1,124,712	3,573,727	1,653,800	3,869,508	885,434	461,049	350,360	280,813
Spain	643,087	1,734,640	418,420	157,217	270,473	1,928,362	211,156	3,694	252	312
Austrian territories	456,968	311,240	285,208	420,192	561,588	1,335,921	1,696,848	1,911,110	1,410,391	1,382,183
Roumania	266,163	124,540	53,468	351,086	384,814	229,808	104,825	158,854	126,629	214,855

Turkey	563,779	296,292	569,709	960,718	866,443	1,026,280	154,833	11,500	4,419	28,299
Egypt	2,361,042	1,271,704	297,928	2,112,738	249,252	461,046	218,236	2,063,718	1,605,437	1,072,550
British North America	2,157,170	4,315,709	4,208,315	4,008,565	2,770,955	3,265,174	2,999,400	5,353,697	4,543,407	3,200,434
United States:										
Atlantic ports	4,188,725	14,636,880	21,085,372	17,206,410	15,105,922	13,973,413	28,666,221	37,015,145	37,690,297	33,168,149
Pacific ports	1,445,024	7,136,230	6,129,640	9,105,741	7,117,441	9,620,592	4,919,959	7,604,474	7,092,813	12,531,807
Chili	1,677,908	1,537,537	2,207,016	802,660	1,012,642	808,703	50,573	1,492,041	1,450,348	1,171,039
British India	161,915	741,330	1,054,380	434,374	3,296,575	6,106,079	1,829,681	889,531	3,230,144	7,338,751
Australasia	556,180	2,091,564	1,156,509	1,265,717	2,842,200	451,102	1,561,000	2,284,653	4,613,353	3,314,540
Other countries	802,113	649,007	310,363	323,073	446,356	596,538	83,690	290,390	127,054	95,619
Total	47,612,890	51,631,197	40,322,693	50,546,621	51,994,433	63,491,429	50,091,583	73,002,110	68,456,814	71,344,659

BARLEY.

Russia	1,755,340	1,119,094	2,010,300	2,685,358	1,547,518	1,499,565	4,827,663	2,473,104	1,491,464	1,167,922
Sweden	357,941	182,004	341,474	463,834	320,490	318,254	460,557	401,024	496,047	229,129
Denmark	4,824,492	650,011	1,363,345	1,187,741	994,417	905,018	1,654,104	212,453	2,118,457	1,376,908
Germany	1,672,577	1,138,737	728,262	1,119,266	431,312	2,592,513	3,150,017	2,600,513	2,636,847	1,602,306
France	6,183,067	1,970,958	2,136,414	2,401,755	1,642,070	1,900,054	459,568	625,680	1,165,175	2,001,182
Roumania	1,218,246	636,606	958,876	439,760	964,543	212,915	1,068,651	1,512,987	417,641	1,857,134
Turkey	499,205	905,146	3,327,078	1,553,537	3,235,653	3,784,906	1,026,863	80,301	837,530	251,904
Egypt	70,033	16,510	48,270	127,663	272,718	220,028	141,306	125,234	59,071
United States	17,656	14,520	32,200	7,708	128,571	807,401	1,084,502	138,521	334,345	273,859
Chili	9	6,553	245,684	700	4,453	60,354	249,147	3,397
Other countries	448,020	200,939	403,574	231,945	235,362	625,050	224,894	296,760	023,333	862,172
Total	15,046,556	9,241,068	11,335,396	11,049,476	9,772,943	12,970,528	14,136,919	11,546,314	11,705,290	9,805,914

OATS.

Russia	2,303,957	4,873,281	5,016,253	6,445,735	4,719,581	7,412,961	6,301,684	7,062,190	7,843,657	5,698,287
Sweden	4,823,713	3,068,647	4,187,672	3,116,672	4,278,023	3,083,578	4,081,140	4,479,287	4,061,822	3,309,974
Denmark	1,067,729	820,508	478,168	294,190	216,906	106,437	289,071	312,895	338,948	160,855
Germany	769,274	201,568	834,628	139,702	314,353	1,281,760	1,645,498	301,874	116,868	66,740
Holland	622,494	294,210	287,413	461,416	306,703	316,643	290,602	151,830	173,244	166,699
France	578,587	237,165	287,633	74,174	12,564	12,340	2,463	32,183	128	13,063
British North America	345,534	764,612	272,702	394,612	1,085,144	604,373	664,283	485,338	738,990	546,214
United States	70	8,725	5,435	142,289	742,566	41,927	40,148	20,645	67,804	7,877
Other counties	1,066,063	239,870	233,483	144,151	93,670	50,000	58,931	119,454	493,281	454,410
Total	11,537,325	11,907,702	11,357,768	12,435,888	11,211,019	12,910,035	12,774,420	13,471,660	13,826,732	10,324,114

IV.—*The quantities and value of wheat, rye, and maize imported, &c.—Continued.*

MAIZE.

Countries.	1872.	1873.	1874.	1875.	1876.	1877.	1878.	1879.	1880.	1881.
	Cwts.	Cwts.	Cwts.	Cwts.	Cwts.	Cwts.	Cwts.	Cwts.	Cwts.	Cwts.
Russia	423,551	1,353,395	508,501	594,115	829,606	199,931	1,023,521	697,626	982,747	754,142
France	10,902	5,703	98,420	268,531	587	4,760	944	58	1,069	7,460
Austrian territories	155,636	131,338	98,781	1,188,707	65,749		30,707	2,346		
Roumania	948,413	1,270,464	357,050	578,502	2,311,548	130,705	1,933,570	2,950,895	1,784,442	6,481,820
Turkey	1,639,615	2,783,100	1,172,715	3,670,053	6,078,732	2,030,697	2,746,378	23,968	166,708	504,611
Egypt	372,001	38,940	12,749	63,100	132,271	43,605		277	15,742	93,565
British North America	3,557,896	1,761,175	1,320,228	873,776	1,872,415	2,013,797	2,829,382	2,026,902	3,342,327	1,592,727
United States	6,940,643	10,762,353	13,454,617	12,068,606	27,065,440	25,577,778	32,877,700	30,470,143	31,087,773	29,714,933
Other countries	443,653	712,963	680,518	1,032,700	761,001	476,545	229,704	57,182	63,894	331,568
Total	24,532,670	18,823,431	17,603,625	20,438,480	39,903,369	30,477,818	41,673,000	30,148,379	37,224,733	33,480,846

RYE.

	1872.	1873.	1874.	1875.	1876.	1877.	1878.	1879.	1880.	1881.
Total	235,422	61,771	470,018	310,103	132,306	241,209	342,395	297,253	126,112	169,218

V.—*Values of imports.*

Description.	1872.	1873.	1874.	1875.	1876.	1877.	1878.	1879.	1880.	1881.
	Dollars.	Dollars.	Dollars.	Dollars.	Dollars.	Dollars.	Dollars.	Dollars.	Dollars.	Dollars.
Wheat	127,532,330	138,843,597	122,815,590	133,879,097	112,795,791	144,003,479	131,504,856	131,130,854	149,017,150	153,449,214
Barley	30,143,568	19,572,636	25,750,048	22,559,302	18,238,109	26,250,726	26,972,541	33,389,944	24,396,805	19,795,491
Oats	30,440,541	23,358,416	24,009,590	20,311,068	22,485,430	24,907,846	22,179,677	21,884,291	24,012,599	18,380,009
Maize	42,205,686	32,347,782	38,414,900	39,515,771	62,106,721	43,690,483	61,295,529	47,782,222	54,325,129	50,652,002
Other kinds of grain	9,010,743	8,888,664	10,614,632	12,082,053	12,731,622	11,934,760	7,892,651	8,308,671	9,075,205	8,377,349
Flour of wheat	19,802,739	28,468,333	27,666,422	23,701,106	23,674,589	33,136,911	33,015,293	41,174,735	43,368,279	44,797,198
Flour of other kinds	163,641	303,535	331,272	296,404	692,985	720,807	2,038,422	2,057,858	2,105,335	709,107

These tables of imports of breadstuffs show how largely Great Britain is dependent upon foreign supplies for food, and the great value of the grain exports of the United States. In round numbers, it has cost Great Britain $275,000,000 a year for foreign cereals during the last ten years, while lately $300,000,000 a year have been spent. The United States have furnished on an average 36 per cent. of the wheat imported, and last year 64 per cent. of the wheat was from the United States.

In maize the percentage for the past ten years is still higher—70 per cent.; within this period the imports of wheat have increased nearly five fold from the United States; barley thirty fold, but decreasing; maize three to four fold. The wheat table shows a decrease in imports from Russia, Germany, and France, and an increase in British Indian grain. Next to the United States, Roumania exports the most maize to Great Britain; France exports the most barley, and Russia the most oats. It would also appear that British North America and British India will in the future be no mean rivals of the United States in wheat exports to Great Britain, but how serious the competition will be depends upon too many unknown factors to be as yet even estimated.

E. A. MERRITT,

Consul-General.

UNITED STATES CONSULATE-GENERAL,
London, September 15, 1882.

THE CROPS OF SCOTLAND.

REPORT BY CONSUL LEONARD, OF LEITH.

The harvest throughout Great Britain this year, with all the drawback of unsettled weather during by-gone months, has proved the best in point of result of any harvest during the past seven years, although a good deal of grain is still outstanding in the backward parts of the country, owing to the broken weather that has prevailed during the past week.

Wheat appears, up to the present time, to be a good fair crop, perhaps rather under, in point of quantity, to the estimated annual average of the years previous to 1875, when the British average in respect to yield was usually taken at about half the yearly national consumption, or about eighty to a hundred million bushels of wheat.

While there is therefore a fair result as to yield this season, it is pretty evident that Great Britain will still have to import from abroad, and that principally from America, at the least a hundred and ten million bushels of wheat or its equivalent amount of flour.

The quality and weight per bushel of the wheat crop is also fair, as, although the bloom has been taken off the wheat to some extent by the large amount of rain which has fallen, the acceptable breezes and frequent sunny days have enabled farmers generally to secure the grain in good condition.

From the beginning of September last year to the opening of this year, wheat fell 24 to 30 cents per bushel in price, and only showed an average price for British wheat of $1.35 per bushel, the quality being poor, while No. 2 red winter of good sound quality made about $1.61 per bushel.

Barley is a good, useful crop this season, though not over one-third of the yield can be considered of choice color or finest malting quality; such at present is $1.13 to $1.28 per bushel.

The great bulk of this crop, although, occasionally a little rough and variable as to color, is pretty dry and of good weight. It will, therefore, be found most useful both by brewers and maltsters. It may bring 90 cents to $1.10 per bushel, weighing 56 pounds, while the remainder of the crop may be worth 75 to 90 cents per bushel, and is well fitted for distillery and milling purposes.

Oats are the crop of the season, being of large bulk and fruitful yield per acre, while they are also of excellent quality and generally of good weight and superior condition. But much of the oat crop still remains exposed in the later and higher districts of the country. The value runs at present from 82 to 97 cents per bushel for best descriptions, and 65 to 80 cents per bushel for ordinary sorts.

Beans are a good crop, well podded, and of sound quality.

Few pears are now grown, and these have suffered to some extent from the wet.

There is a large bulk of straw from all the cereals this year, and the hay crop is bulky and of good quality.

Potatoes will give a good yield. In the Lothian counties farmers are still busy with the potatoes, but as the crop is gathered the disease is found to be making serious ravages. Prices have risen slightly; but $17 per ton, equal to 46 cents per bushel, appears to be the most that can be realized for marketable potatoes, while for diseased ones, fit for feeding cattle or pigs, farmers are glad to get $6 per ton, or about 16 cents per bushel.

Turnips, according to all accounts, will turn out, in some places at least, the largest crop within the memory of the present generation.

The roots are sound and of good quality, but owing to their abundance they fetch but a poor price, and only those farmers get the full advantage of the crop who can afford to buy lean sheep or cattle to fatten on it.

Owing to the demand thus created the price of stock rules high. Turnips, it is believed, will rise in value in the event of frost being experienced.

Although the abundance of the harvest in America is evidently very great, and it is obvious that supplies of wheat and flour from that quarter will be large all through the season, it remains to be seen whether the potato disease may not yet affect food prices to a greater or lesser extent.

It is very likely to do so to some moderate degree further on, but, meanwhile, as that root crop is somewhat pressed on the market, it may rather have an opposite effect for the present, as the cheapness at which potatoes are offered may materially affect the consumption of breadstuffs and thus interfere with the regular demand on millers and flour merchants. Shipments from America continue small, and the sales for early delivery are also limited.

These circumstances, taken together with the estimated loss on potatoes here, and the near approach of winter in the Upper Baltic stopping St. Petersburg shipments at an early date, may help to strengthen the tone if not improve the prices of wheat in the British market.

J. A. LEONARD,
Consul.

UNITED STATES CONSULATE,
Leith, October 19, 1882.

CEREALS OF SWITZERLAND.

REPORT BY CONSUL ADAMS, OF GENEVA.

Upon the receipt of the circular I wrote to the federal bureau of statistics and the department of commerce and agriculture at Berne, and at the same time to Mr. F. Demoll, of this city, who in turn wrote to the department above named.

I inclose with this translations of letters received from the bureau of statistics, and from Mr. Demoll, which will suffice to show the difficulty of collecting information of the kind required in this country.

LYELL T. ADAMS,
Consul.

UNITED STATES CONSULATE,
Geneva, August 3, 1882.

Mr. Demoll to Consul Adams.

GENEVA, *July* 31, 1882.

On receipt of your letter of the 9th instant, I applied to the federal department of agriculture for the information you require upon the cultivation of cereals in Switzerland. As I intimated to you in our last interview, no documents exist which afford an answer to your questions, and I do not think that further researches would yield an appreciable result.

The secretary of the department informs me that in 1860 it was estimated that 380,000 hectares were cultivated for cereals, and he believes that since then the area has greatly decreased, judging from the growth of the trade in cattle and dairy products. He sends me tables of Swiss imports and exports for ten years, which I think will be of little use to you, as the home consumption of cereals does not appear.

Regretting my inability to answer you more fully, I am, &c.,

F. DEMOLL.

Mr. LYELL T. ADAMS,
Consul, &c.

CEREALS IN ITALY.

REPORT BY CONSUL-GENERAL RICHMOND, OF ROME.

I have the honor to transmit herewith eight tabular statements, in obedience to the call for statistical information as to the cereal crop of Italy, contained in circular from the Department of State, dated 1882.

The crops from 1872 to 1879, inclusive, and the areas under cultivation for that period, are an average statement made up by the government on the basis of the crops and the areas of 1872, 1873, and 1874.

Beginning with 1880 a new system was adopted, and for that year and 1881 a more precise statement is given.

For the statistics I am under great obligations to Professor Luigi Bodio, chief of the bureau of statistics, and also to Mr. Vincenzo Magaldi, secretary to the minister of agriculture and commerce.

LEWIS RICHMOND,
Consul-General.

UNITED STATES CONSULATE-GENERAL,
Rome, August 3, 1882.

CEREALS IN ITALY.

TABLE 1.—*Average annual area under cultivation from 1872 to 1879, inclusive.*

Provinces.	Wheat.	Indian corn.	Rye and barley.		Rice.
	Acres.	*Acres.*	*Acres.*	*Acres.*	*Acres.*
Piedmont	465,441	331,149	122,720	28,961	181,922
Lombardy	563,850	610,054	101,707	52,334	249,162
Venetia	562,701	637,904	76,140	68,821	79,682
Liguria	203,174	63,013	11,986	2,116	......
Emilia	1,443,915	550,561	27,384	32,799	50,914
Marches and Umbria	1,067,013	504,656	36,180	34,715	......
Tuscany	997,689	304,852	29,279	107,808	1,185
Rome	395,000	86,326	2,625	19,760	......
Southern Adriatic Provinces	1,880,648	435,246	214,527	275,158	172
Southern Mediterranean Provinces	2,570,200	679,200	195,151	206,830	140
Sicily	610,667	4,638	310,555	10,270	1,183
Sardinia	125,489	5,656	52,297	......	......
Total	10,855,189	4,213,256	1,184,651	939,574	573,360

TABLE 2.—*Average areas under cultivation in 1880 and 1881.*

Provinces.	Wheat.	Indian corn.	Rye and barley.	Oats.	Rice.
	Acres.	*Acres.*	*Acres.*	*Acres.*	*Acres.*
Piedmont	465,441	343,169	122,730	28,961	182,120
Lombardy	491,618	745,161	110,574	52,334	213,061
Venetia	559,642	637,904	73,440	68,821	40,176
Liguria	203,174	63,032	9,137	2,116	......
Emilia	1,196,915	560,561	27,384	32,799	60,421
Marches and Umbria	1,070,907	509,667	37,949	36,659	......
Tuscany	995,654	305,687	25,746	107,808	1,185
Rome	395,200	86,326	2,205	19,760	......
Southern Adriatic Provinces	1,894,295	435,246	180,033	277,905	172
Southern Mediterranean Provinces	2,570,200	693,862	183,637	329,819	74
Sicily	1,397,790	4,628	320,857	10,010	1,479
Sardinia	309,957	5,606	53,297	......	......
Total	11,550,792	4,190,919	1,146,911	967,084	538,688

TABLE 3.—*Average of crops harvested per year, from 1872 to 1879, inclusive.*

Provinces.	Wheat	Indian corn.	Rye and barley.	Oats.	Rice.
	Bushels.	*Bushels.*	*Bushels.*	*Bushels.*	*Bushels.*
Piedmont	5,184,497	7,899,694	1,654,083	567,061	9,007,908
Lombardy	7,911,002	13,875,187	1,612,231	1,017,113	12,066,139
Venetia	7,152,586	14,202,535	1,104,207	1,340,310	3,452,446
Liguria	1,939,355	1,176,331	157,440	37,048	......
Emilia	15,892,114	11,868,130	369,207	601,727	2,326,703
Marches and Umbria	11,674,725	9,886,166	503,181	565,974	......
Tuscany	12,548,077	6,044,974	391,594	2,167,101	40,920
Rome	4,331,500	1,789,637	30,570	506,000	......
Southern Adriatic Provinces	20,514,042	7,700,086	3,497,073	5,574,598	5,380
Southern Mediterranean Provinces	31,736,848	13,104,014	2,889,068	5,017,683	5,054
Sicily	17,217,662	103,470	3,574,487	161,326	39,883
Sardinia	2,855,212	77,000	903,732	......	......
Total	138,957,520	57,107,424	16,706,873	18,455,941	26,944,433

TABLE 4.—*Crops harvested in 1880 and 1881.*

Provinces.	Wheat.		Indian corn.	
	1880.	1881.	1880.	1881.
	Bushels.	*Bushels.*	*Bushels.*	*Bushels.*
Piedmont	5,637,182	4,814,639	7,184,596	4,596,405
Lombardy	7,796,687	7,698,801	13,685,218	8,527,554
Venetia	7,508,766	7,147,967	12,397,720	8,264,212
Liguria	2,055,556	1,573,330	836,624	639,567
Emilia	18,727,792	14,415,531	11,681,408	7,745,080
Marches and Umbria	14,644,269	8,787,504	10,046,316	6,125,139
Tuscany	14,551,554	8,708,515	5,441,515	3,379,759
Rome	3,966,764	2,427,646	1,148,160	1,148,160
Southern Adriatic Provinces	27,061,117	15,288,493	8,357,791	4,787,810
Southern Mediterranean Provinces	38,390,154	18,204,219	10,184,330	9,838,754
Sicily	21,751,692	9,499,864	72,561	89,364
Sardinia	2,723,621	2,142,558	44,649	57,263
Total	164,818,804	100,708,461	81,074,888	55,199,097

Provinces.	Rye and barley.		Oats.		Rice.	
	1880.	1881.	1880.	1881.	1880.	1881.
	Bushels.	*Bushels.*	*Bushels.*	*Bushels.*	*Bushels.*	*Bushels.*
Piedmont	1,651,234	1,264,675	578,325	430,633	9,407,355	7,031,914
Lombardy	1,477,375	1,441,233	924,841	954,258	12,310,661	10,835,467
Venetia	988,718	960,393	1,304,688	1,264,252	3,116,624	3,132,778
Liguria	143,339	122,771	31,429	29,452	....	....
Emilia	402,171	337,790	658,545	611,261	2,369,851	2,098,890
Marches and Umbria	546,742	385,254	587,671	370,465	....	....
Tuscany	387,715	286,495	1,896,484	1,507,457	44,602	33,759
Rome	40,693	22,733	692,140	384,320	....	....
Southern Adriatic Provinces	4,616,397	2,599,025	6,038,648	3,778,255	7,606	3,773
Southern Mediterranean Provinces	3,133,260	1,713,472	6,275,558	3,968,205	2,849	4,182
Sicily	5,057,721	2,874,349	191,231	116,478	38,007	29,447
Sardinia	781,421	776,655	....	....	....	....
Total	18,626,188	13,784,815	19,089,560	13,389,036	27,297,555	23,170,210

TABLE 5.—*Imports and exports of wheat from 1872 to 1881, inclusive.*

IMPORTS.

Countries where from.	1872.	1873.	1874.	1875.	1876.	1877.	1878.	1870.	1880.	1881.
	Tons.	*Tons.*	*Tons.*	*Tons.*	*Tons.*	*Tons.*	*Tons.*	*Tons.*	*Tons.*	*Tons.*
England	3,810	3,119	42,157	6,650	8,903	523	165	1,127	171	1,352
France	14,315	26,600	30,520	17,416	13,978	8,154	9,914	11,504	5,081	4,549
Austria	10,740	1,798	5,962	581	10,157	5,510	15,233	32,640	2,143	643
Germany							512			
Switzerland	474			45		1	60			
Russia	209,260	132,636	134,629	195,349	126,596	72,164	200,462	287,447	180,505	78,968
Spain, Gibraltar, and Portugal		1,684							11	1,198
United States and Canada		275					3,242	6,299	3,362	118
South America								721		
Greece and Malta	17,095	5,388	16,633	11,687	9,506	7,221	6,896	6,408	4,360	8,899
European Turkey	34,006	84,031	191,599	102,338	185,234	133,185	86,996	127,991	41,370	33,018
Asiatic Turkey							15,247	13,416	6,525	17,873
Egypt	1,646	871	976	961	3,074	683	14,263	11,860	5,002	1,375
Tunis and Tripoli	12,347	37,591	16,988	7,833	4,935	2,881	14,440	6,587	2,125	3,088
Algiers							365	4,595	2,182	4,000
Other African countries							1,232		1,030	
English possessions in Asia							86	21	507	
Other countries							18,963	27,256		7,205
Totals	361,143	296,193	288,460	342,910	362,413	231,622	381,545	538,215	238,204	162,506

EXPORTS.

Countries where sent.	1872.	1873.	1874.	1875.	1876.	1877.	1878.	1870.	1880.	1881.
	Tons.	*Tons.*	*Tons.*	*Tons.*	*Tons.*	*Tons.*	*Tons.*	*Tons.*	*Tons.*	*Tons.*
England	24,230	10,737	271	8,705	23,572	22,623	2,644	10,851	1,750	143
France	34,327	35,665	11,403	9,634	18,646	29,924	43,489	9,484	44,805	57,819
Austria	18,767	45,001	24,985	39,529	33,686	21,560	12,882		32,844	33,475
Germany										
Switzerland	5,253	5,337	7,037	8,435	6,340	4,355	5,510	4,669	7,039	6,480
Spain, Gibraltar, and Portugal	714		201	120	108		53			
Belgium	123					209				
Holland	225	177								
Central America	303									
South America	1,776		184							
Greece and Malta	245			32		24		7		38
European Turkey	363		8	46	6	187	137	20	976	402
Egypt	81			4			39			88
Tunis and Tripoli	806				13	187	21			
Algiers							404			
Other countries									720	561
Totals	67,363	116,937	44,299	66,505	82,371	80,069	65,211	25,034	89,104	104,457

* Tons of 2,000 pounds.

TABLE 6.—*Imports and exports of Indian corn, Saracen grain, rye, and barley from 1872 to 1881, inclusive.*

IMPORTS.

Countries where from.	1872.	1873.	1874.	1875.	1876.	1877.	1878.	1879.	1880.	1881.
	Tons.	*Tons.*	*Tons.*	*Tons.*	*Tons.*	*Tons.*	*Tons.*	*Tons.*	*Tons.*	*Tons.*
England	1,378	699	6,904	3,354	814	684	376	2,120	1,148	819
France	3,177	3,825	7,141	1,027	1,659	3,580	3,723	5,404	5,700	5,798
Austria	14,127	5,410	28,810	2,356	5,594	13,661	20,279	40,234	25,980	14,956
Germany			35		341	46	70	321	170	269
Switzerland	81			41	133	58		127		
Russia	20,842	2,448	6,616	2,871	1,160	6,649	29,041	97,863	163,181	61,748
United States and Canada		2,117	5,926		683	16,984	23,108	44,610	111,574	23,304
South America						611	10,139	2,347	11,698	10,024
Greece and Malta		953	8,988	1,005	705	1,831	2,342	462	10,008	31,545
European Turkey	7,870	21,810	65,800	4,566	3,315	19,374	37,476	84,397	30,198	1,126
Asiatic Turkey						30	238	938	1,213	238
Egypt	831	1,391	2,256	2,786	1,110	357	72	667	4,185	183
Tunis and Tripoli	1,317		7,541			48	779	2,143	586	
Other countries			104				5,680	11,167		
Totals	49,613	38,653	140,021	18,616	15,523	63,813	133,832	291,981	361,641	140,310

EXPORTS.

Countries where sent.	1872.	1873.	1874.	1875.	1876.	1877.	1878.	1879.	1880.	1881.
	Tons.	*Tons.*	*Tons.*	*Tons.*	*Tons.*	*Tons.*	*Tons.*	*Tons.*	*Tons.*	*Tons.*
England	25,703	29,084	8,930	48,615	23,976	17,198	8,963	2,388	10,001	1,571
France	16,050	22,749	12,849	42,635	43,163	25,164	27,595	14,675	18,204	14,060
Austria	33,174	40,595	30,561	40,258	38,407	24,727	18,910	20,506	16,835	18,387
Germany				13	118	227	61	329	67	353
Switzerland	12,003	7,427	11,083	10,060	22,136	12,847	10,422	8,867	7,240	6,049
Spain, Gibraltar, and Portugal	876	2,716	2,105	2,802	9,953	1,701	13,515	9,714	2,119	1,055
Belgium	733	486	28	470	1,705	2,435	1,980	1,988	2,355	2,375
Holland		147		64	570	87	253	114	1,953	
United States and Canada	331	17	25	461	424	210	1,614	1,269	116	55
South America	37	1,076	40	30	41	626	3,417	2,081	2,560	236
Greece and Malta	197	67		14	22	140	17	132	92	1,600
European Turkey	118	100	37	111	11	436	112	248	195	86
Egypt	224	494	23	52	74	87	242	164	260	205
Tunis and Tripoli		1,943			28	1,187	550	91	753	293
Algiers										
Other countries				65	46	56				42
Totals	89,148	106,961	65,690	145,650	141,274	87,128	88,381	63,125	62,863	46,357

* Tons of 2,000 pounds,

TABLE 7.—*Imports and exports of oats from 1872 to 1881, inclusive.*

IMPORTS.

Countries where from.	1872.	1873.	1874.	1875.	1876.	1877.	1878.	1879.	1880.	1881.
	Tons.	*Tons.*	*Tons.*	*Tons.*	*Tons.*	*Tons.*	*Tons.*	*Tons.*	*Tons.*	*Tons.*
England	89					267				
France	203	102	564	167	720	55	23	59	20	35
Austria	55	1,380	12,310	51	1,076	1,780	937	844	2,360	3,326
Switzerland	34			2,453	28	7			12	56
Russia		1,040	1,970	208	844	1,146	410	484	7,953	1,921
Greece and Malta			887	324	145	19	101	14	25	67
Turkey in Europe	217	553	3,855	2,312	782	418	329	1,648	1,583	1,088
Other countries			24			3		56	137	158
Totals	608	3,075	19,610	5,517	4,395	3,695	1,800	3,006	11,978	6,649

EXPORTS.

Countries where sent.	1872.	1873.	1874.	1875.	1876.	1877.	1878.	1879.	1880.	1881.
	Tons.	*Tons.*	*Tons.*	*Tons.*	*Tons.*	*Tons.*	*Tons.*	*Tons.*	*Tons.*	*Tons.*
England	3,910	1,298	2,088	5,082	9,626	5,629	12,994	2,747	3,736	1,105
France	10,995	8,536								4,584
Austria	3,173	1,329	313	998	630	242	688	477	453	140
Switzerland	1,193	1,943	3,010	312	1,206	455	679	1,887	554	894
Greece and Malta				4			86	17		
Other counties		4,047				1	17	3		
Totals	19,271	18,014	5,641	6,426	11,462	6,327	14,464	6,131	4,745	6,763

* Tons of 2,000 pounds.

TABLE 8.—*Imports and exports of rice from 1872 to 1881 inclusive.*

IMPORTS.

Countries where from.	1872.	1873.	1874.	1875.	1876.	1877.	1878.	1879.	1880.	1881.
	Tons.	*Tons.*	*Tons.*	*Tons.*	*Tons.*	*Tons.*	*Tons.*	*Tons.*	*Tons.*	*Tons.*
England	353	23,770	20,420	8,214	12,195	13,099	6,288	17,812	22,991	19,294
France	2,455	196	183	86	192	255	101	428	1,113	113
Austria	1,018	918	1,617	936	1,759	3,671	1,570	364	614	690
Germany								195	113	
United States and Canada								626		
South America	5,504									
Greece and Malta			76			1	108	788	1,738	844
Turkey in Europe		542	1,185	408	2,682		608			
Egypt			666		2,191	1	2,721	22	32,045	
English possessions in Asia							1,799	8,080	52	4,250
Other countries	29									
Totals	9,420	27,426	24,147	9,044	20,631	17,927	13,175	28,315	58,066	25,181

EXPORTS.

Countries where sent.	1872.	1873.	1874.	1875.	1876.	1877.	1878.	1879.	1880.	1881.
	Tons.	*Tons.*	*Tons.*	*Tons.*	*Tons.*	*Tons.*	*Tons.*	*Tons.*	*Tons.*	*Tons.*
England	6,557	2,745	741	1,196	1,748	3,920	1,320	201	513	1,535
France	29,173	33,738	30,572	30,047	27,143	13,274	25,856	30,707	30,276	28,641
Austria	18,664	24,843	18,528	14,987	16,380	11,784	23,518	18,053	20,396	22,011
Germany	43	20	439	247	253	208		41	251	44
Switzerland	2,457	2,870	3,763	3,145	1,076	3,325	1,404	2,180	2,204	3,220
Russia	14,274	8,676	5,707	2,621	100	286	311	215	170	228
Spain, Gibraltar, and Portugal	188		186	20			613	182	3,061	
United States and Canada	8,974	92		114	92	720		14		286
South and Central America	106	70	6,910	9,639	4,048	3,300	3,927	4,927	5,304	10,208
Greece and Malta	184	495	3,050	6,914	5,274	4,411	4,648	1,877	767	4,257
Turkey in Europe	1,016	96	4,082	10,868	1,872	5,890	17,297	17,570	12,748	20,270
Egypt	1,769		2,083	2,715	154	835	275	445	630	1,055
Tunis and Tripoli	24	108	159	13	216	48	256	231	181	439
Other countries				96	89		67	534	7,279	25
Totals	87,448	73,774	76,229	61,552	59,957	48,240	79,518	83,176	83,780	92,619

* Tons of 2,000 pounds.

CEREALS OF AUSTRIA-HUNGARY.

REPORT BY CONSUL-GENERAL WEAVER, OF VIENNA.

In conformity with instructions contained in Department circular of May 31, 1882, I have to transmit herewith certain tabular statements showing the production of and commerce in cereals and other grain in Austria-Hungary, during the decade 1871–'80. The tables have been carefully compiled from data obtained from official sources. The imports and exports could not be procured for the years 1871–'74, not having been prepared in the form desired previous to the years given, while those embraced in the tables have been compiled from the "Auswartiger Handel der Oestereichisch-Ungarischen Monarchie" for 1875–'80, by Joseph Pizzala, of Vienna.

The quantities and values, as far as practicable, have been reduced to acres, bushels, and dollars, at the following rates, viz: In the tables of productions the hectare and hectoliter have been calculated at, respectively, 2.471 acres and 2.84 bushels, while in the tables of imports and exports the florin has been estimated at 41 cents, the metrical centner at 220 pounds, and 60 pounds of wheat, but 56 of rye and maize per bushel, in conformity with sections 2919 and 3570 of the Revised Statutes of the United States.

I would, in this connection, call the serious attention of the Department to the unnecessary labor imposed upon consuls by insisting that quantities and values in commercial reports should be reduced to certain denominations possibly more familiar to the general reader in the United States, but no more convenient to merchants, statisticians, and others consulting these reports. The amount of labor involved in these reductions is simply enormous, if they are sufficiently accurate to be of any value, and since the metrical system has been adopted by most European nations and authorized by the United States, the question arises whether the Department might not materially aid in the adoption of the more convenient weights and measures of the metrical system by directing that commercial reports, when found in such weights and measures, might be transmitted without further reduction.

AVERAGE ANNUAL PRODUCTION OF GRAIN.

From Tables I and II the following interesting *résumé* of the total annual average production of grain during the decade 1871–'80 has been made:

Grain.	Austria.	Hungary.	Total.
	Bushels.	*Bushels.*	*Bushels.*
Wheat	36,431,746	60,869,534	97,301,280
Rye	69,084,580	31,674,197	101,658,777
Maize	16,965,299	60,935,652	77,900,951
Millet, spelt, maslin	3,149,509	7,908,492	11,058,092
Oats	87,085,720	41,839,538	129,825,258
Barley	45,554,005	34,207,315	79,761,320
Buckwheat	7,747,662	396,503	8,144,165
Total	267,818,611	237,831,232	505,649,843

In connection with the foregoing table it should be remarked that maslin, being a mixture of wheat and rye, composed about one-fourth of the whole amount, while millet constituted probably 50 per cent. of the whole in Austria; while in Hungary about 90 per cent. of the totals put down to millet, spelt, and maslin belongs to the last.

AVERAGE ANNUAL GRAIN ACREAGE.

Notwithstanding the most diligent search through every source of information at my command, the acreage for Austria could not be found excepting for the year 1880, for the statistical year-book of the Ministry of Agriculture and that of the Central Statistical Commission omit, excepting for 1880, the desired data. This is so much the more surprising, as the year-books of Hungary give these data in a most complete, convenient, and commendable form.

From Table III, therefore, we obtain the following résumé, giving the acreage of Austria for 1880, and the average in Hungary during the decade 1871-'80:

Grain.	Austria, 1880.	Hungary, average for 1871-'80.	Total.
	Acres.	Acres.	Acres.
Wheat	2,356,349	5,678,770	8,035,119
Rye	4,548,721	3,077,666	7,626,387
Maize	828,151	4,254,581	5,082,731
Millet, spelt, maslin	228,469	733,832	962,301
Oats	4,436,789	2,631,346	7,068,135
Barley	2,666,118	2,342,266	5,008,384
Buckwheat	420,386	78,914	499,300
Total	15,484,083	18,797,375	34,282,358

It may be remarked that the crop and acreage of Austria for 1880 was officially estimated as follows, counting 100 as an average, viz: Wheat, 111 and 103; rye, 91 and 95; maize, 108 and 107; oats, 105 and 99; and barley, 112 and 110; so that the foregoing table may be considered a fair approximation of the annual average acreage of Austria-Hungary in 1871-'80.

AVERAGE ANNUAL YIELD PER ACRE.

The average yield per acre for the several classes of grain in Austria-Hungary, by a simple mathematical computation, becomes as follows, given in bushels per acre:

Grain.	Austria in 1880.	Hungary in 1871-'80.	Total.
Wheat	17.2	10.7	12.1
Rye	14.2	10.3	13.3
Maize	20.4	14.3	15.3
Millet, spelt, maslin	14.7	10.8	11.5
Oats	29.2	12.1	18.4
Barley	19.0	14.6	15.9
Buckwheat	18.9	5.0	16.3
Average	17.9	12.6	14.7

AVERAGE IMPORTS AND EXPORTS COMPARED.

By comparing the average imports and exports of cereals and flour during the years 1875–'80, as shown in Tables V to XI, inclusive, we have the following results:

Articles.	Imports.	Exports.	Balance.
Wheat..bushels..	6, 548, 772	9, 395, 517	2, 846, 745
Rye...do....	2, 522, 765	2, 467, 732	55, 033
Maize...do ...	6, 685, 464	3, 419, 912	3, 265. 552
Flour .... tons..	54, 136	161, 577	107, 441

It would appear, therefore, that Austria-Hungary, out of an average annual wheat crop of 97,00.',000 bushels, exported in 1875 a clear annual average of 2,846,745 bushels and 107,441 tons flour, equivalent approximately to about seven per centum of the crop.

Table XIII shows in a succinct form the imports and exports of grain and flour during the decade of 1871–'80, and cannot fail to interest those seeking information of that nature. This table is taken almost without change from Mr. Pizzala's valuable report, above alluded to, and I am therefore at liberty to praise it without stint.

JAMES RILEY WEAVER,
Consul-General.

UNITED STATES CONSULATE-GENERAL,
Vienna, August 16, 1882.

TABULAR STATEMENTS SHOWING THE PRODUCTION AND COMMERCE OF GRAIN AND FLOUR IN AUSTRIA-HUNGARY DURING THE DECADE 1871–'80.

I.—*Tabular statement showing the production of cereals and other grain in Austria during the decade 1871–'80.*

[Reported in bushels reduced at the rate of 2.84 bushels per hectoliter.]

Years.	Wheat.	Rye.	Maize.	Millet, spelt, and maslin.	Total cereals.	Oats.	Barley.	Buckwheat.	Total grain.
	Bushels.	*Bushels.*	*Bushels.*	*Bushels.*	*Bushels.*	*Bushels.*	*Bushels.*	*Bushels.*	*Bushels.*
1871	36,208,403	74,613,611	11,050,907	1,024,248	122,985,309	61,877,859	46,523,902	8,306,781	269,693,911
1872	31,882,234	66,713,772	26,268,350	1,055,071	125,917,477	99,214,398	49,324,631	9,824,398	284,080,740
1873	28,530,419	69,452,592	15,242,680	610,368	113,856,079	76,200,724	45,152,458	6,700,085	241,909,346
1874	41,332,328	80,751,330	16,449,211	4,564,331	143,117,200	82,596,853	49,484,412	7,780,759	283,079,224
1875	30,913,811	65,601,790	17,247,533	3,941,033	117,704,167	72,601,970	37,116,099	6,233,990	233,658,226
1876	35,077,584	60,811,429	16,808,025	4,320,713	117,017,751	93,951,716	51,601,003	7,794,149	270,364,618
1877	39,898,533	69,519,940	14,600,332	3,847,223	127,866,028	86,082,774	39,230,717	6,262,347	250,450,866
1878	45,291,433	84,563,828	19,293,025	4,884,464	153,972,770	93,178,993	48,524,595	6,748,239	309,424,597
1879	34,496,346	62,432,436	15,491,916	3,209,006	116,629,704	86,339,743	37,695,024	8,089,239	248,763,710
1880	40,618,333	64,384,873	17,203,016	4,039,522	126,245,744	92,812,279	50,578,213	7,026,638	277,562,874
Annual average	36,431,746	69,984,580	16,965,299	3,149,699	120,531,224	87,985,720	45,554,005	7,747,662	267,818,611

II.—*Tabular statement showing the production of cereals and other grain in Hungary during the decade 1871–'80.*

[Reported in bushels reduced at the rate of 2.84 bushels per hectoliter.]

Years.	Wheat.	Rye.	Maize.	Millet, spelt, and maslin.	Total cereals.	Oats.	Barley.	Buckwheat.	Total grain.
	Bushels.	*Bushels.*	*Bushels.*	*Bushels.*	*Bushels.*	*Bushels.*	*Bushels.*	*Bushels.*	*Bushels.*
1871	45,125,823	38,571,050	34,998,268	8,507,106	127,202,270	40,672,740	34,806,917	524,082	202,645,995
1872	44,202,785	31,581,978	50,815,239	7,199,882	133,799,904	43,353,270	30,492,823	440,225	208,086,222
1873	39,976,285	18,177,760	31,762,281	5,314,119	98,230,451	35,290,021	28,114,801	377,290	162,012,572
1874	61,342,888	34,636,108	21,590,455	8,803,517	126,412,966	30,844,958	36,350,421	586,096	203,200,443
1875	48,970,898	29,459,425	79,910,568	7,880,495	160,607,386	22,293,340	21,609,579	308,523	210,758,828
1876	51,710,098	15,373,281	65,229,006	6,050,488	138,362,871	39,346,530	31,571,633	479,718	209,760,652
1877	76,971,613	37,963,487	54,244,102	7,970,619	177,149,827	40,145,640	34,485,233	282,520	252,063,129
1878	108,706,643	51,996,040	102,946,992	11,016,797	274,666,472	60,216,270	47,454,207	379,276	382,716,225
1879	52,257,703	51,780,931	64,009,415	7,639,554	150,207,663	36,183,285	26,222,305	320,465	212,763,718
1880	79,390,541	34,471,900	98,850,136	8,696,352	221,408,949	61,709,414	50,959,332	266,845	334,344,540
Annual average	60,869,534	31,674,197	60,935,653	7,908,493	161,387,876	41,839,538	34,207,315	390,503	237,831,232

III.—*Tabular statement showing the area of each cereal crop and other grain in Hungary for the decade 1871-'80.*

[Quantities reduced to acres at the rate of 2.471 acres per hectare.]

Years.	Wheat.	Rye.	Maize.	Millet, spelt, and maslin.	Total cereals.	Oats.	Barley.	Buckwheat.	Total grain.
	Acres.	*Acres.*	*Acres.*	*Acres.*	*Acres.*	*Acres.*	*Acres.*	*Acres.*	*Acres.*
1871	4,654,311	3,148,336	3,446,759	722,714	12,642,120	2,403,854	2,147,250	64,008	16,656,892
1872	4,382,586	3,051,634	3,651,419	775,080	12,502,529	2,540,359	2,179,649	57,150	17,299,736
1873	5,293,463	3,203,834	3,791,171	725,089	13,013,555	2,429,784	229,091	56,544	17,829,976
1874	5,343,137	2,940,228	3,550,869	665,826	13,215,240	2,509,687	340,909	82,982	18,250,088
1875	4,661,629	2,975,963	4,312,042	725,557	13,751,933	2,412,089	244,510	78,256	18,463,815
1876	5,432,139	3,425,602	5,446,161	790,774	15,025,362	2,463,331	104,729	87,076	21,510,698
1877	5,971,414	3,494,610	4,467,181	676,293	14,086,208	2,686,208	250,183	76,848	19,150,360
1878	6,184,332	3,557,625	4,452,026	775,308	14,855,145	2,852,228	471,138	81,835	20,259,003
1879	6,090,816	3,020,600	4,441,118	701,352	14,365,145	2,640,358	425,511	91,713	19,608,760
1880	5,368,152	2,662,216	4,009,535	655,100	13,908,072	2,514,645	437,640	108,161	18,946,524
Average	5,678,770	3,077,066	4,254,561	735,862	13,744,849	2,641,396	2,342,206	78,914	18,797,375

IV.—*Tabular statement showing the area of each cereal crop and other grain in Austria for the year 1880.*

[Quantities reduced to acres at the rate of 2.471 acres per hectare.]

Year.	Wheat.	Rye.	Maize.	Millet and maslin	Total cereals.	Oats.	Barley.	Buckwheat.	Total grain.
	Acres.	*Acres.*	*Acres.*	*Acres.*	*Acres.*	*Acres.*	*Acres.*	*Acres.*	*Acres.*
1880	2,536,340	4,548,721	828,121	225,169	7,961,690	4,436,780	2,666,118	429,386	15,484,083

V.—*Tabular statement showing the quantity and value of wheat imported into Austria-Hungary, and from or through which countries, during the years 1875-'80.*

[Quantities given in bushels at the rate of 3⅔ bushels per metrical centner of 100 kilograms.]

Years.	Quantity.	Value.	Countries from or through which imported.							
			Roumania.	Germany.	Russia.	Italy.	Servia and Turkey.	Switzerland.	Trieste.	Fiume and other ports.
	Bushels.		*Bushels.*	*Bushels.*	*Bushels.*	*Bushels.*	*Bushels.*	*Bushels.*	*Bushels.*	*Bushels.*
1875........	3,780,278	$4,015,950	33,238	1,559,842	73,960	932,789	38,273	8	613,906	537,262
1876........	4,261,132	5,360,340	575,915	1,158,447	68,468	654,797	19,547	3,004	973,720	807,235
1877........	5,317,305	7,567,370	2,528,636	1,139,593	100,760	490,996	34,217	1,866	453,820	567,417
1878........	5,406,152	6,637,490	2,381,978	1,170,041	163,511	498,504	1,324	91	485,984	709,719
1879........	8,602,202	9,079,860	3,098,128	1,364,832	2,043,745	522,828	384,663	550	531,304	656,154
1880........	11,925,562	13,974,440	4,822,084	1,064,466	2,276,208	615,747	687,834	5,695	683,089	1,770,439
Average	6,548,772	7,772,575	2,239,997	1,241,370	797,775	618,443	194,310	1,869	623,657	841,371

70 A——4

VI.—*Tabular statement showing the quantity and value of wheat exported from Austria-Hungary, and to or through which countries, during the years 1875–'80.*

[Quantities given in bushels at the rate of 3⅔ bushels per metrical centner of 100 kilograms.]

Years.	Quantity.	Value.	Countries to or through which exported.					
			Germany.	Italy.	Montenegro, Servia, and Turkey.	Other countries.	Trieste.	Fiume and other ports
	Bushels.		Bushels.	Bushels.	Bushels.	Bushels.	Bushels.	Bushels.
1875	3,685,385	$4,532,960	3,379,181	8,487	1,909	18,434	266,040	11,325
1876	4,395,947	5,775,670	4,233,914	20,534	608	22,926	116,045	1,870
1877	13,661,846	22,146,970	10,630,274	223,933	16,275	19,961	2,540,915	230,486
1878	18,285,921	19,312,640	11,272,462	382,825	70,884	21,889	1,187,351	350,510
1879	13,946,596	17,924,790	12,358,608	775,030	7,117	45,887	747,577	12,267
1880	7,397,405	10,743,230	7,099,979	40,945	6,710	36,574	167,574	45,623
Average	9,395,517	13,406,043	8,162,418	241,967	17,251	27,612	817,585	108,664

VII.—*Tabular statement showing the quantity and value of rye imported into Austria-Hungary, and from or through which countries, during the years 1875–'80.*

[Quantities given in bushels at the rate of 3.93 bushels per metrical centner of 100 kilograms.]

Years.	Quantity.	Value.	Countries from or through which imported.			
			Germany.	Russia.	Roumania.	All others.
	Bushels.		Bushels.	Bushels.	Bushels	Bushels.
1875	1,140,832	$928,240	909,602	56,855	18,600	155,766
1876	1,438,789	1,350,950	838,017	110,115	274,161	216,496
1877	2,553,989	2,797,840	1,719,225	246,207	394,772	193,785
1878	2,214,370	1,847,870	1,542,226	240,740	365,765	56,639
1879	3,676,546	2,301,330	1,469,199	1,503,260	548,675	95,412
1880	4,112,065	3,860,970	1,296,393	1,859,035	638,094	318,543
Average	2,522,765	2,181,200	1,295,777	680,869	373,346	172,773

VIII.—*Tabular statement showing the quantity and value of rye exported from Austria-Hungary, and to or through which countries, during the years 1875–'80.*

[Quantities given in bushels at the rate of 3.93 bushels per metrical centner of 100 kilograms.]

Years.	Quantity.	Value.	Countries to or through which exported.		
			Germany.	All others.	Trieste.
	Bushels.		Bushels.	Bushels	Bushels.
1875	2,927,343	$2,534,620	2,918,139	9,141	63
1876	2,804,452	3,145,110	2,798,860	5,572	
1877	1,873,431	2,198,830	1,849,254	1,513	22,664
1878	1,739,088	1,542,010	1,607,394	33,696	97,998
1879	2,938,327	2,298,870	2,892,311	32,917	13,099
1880	2,523,771	2,830,230	2,502,294	15,590	5,887
Average	2,467,732	2,424,945	2,428,042	16,405	23,285

IX.—*Tabular statement showing the quantity and value of maize imported into Austria-Hungary, and from or through which countries, during the years 1875-'80.*

[Quantities given in bushels at the rate of 3.93 bushels per metrical centner of 100 kilograms.]

Countries from or through which imported.

Years.	Quantity.	Value.	Roumania.	Italy.	Russia.	Servia and Turkey.	All others.	Trieste.	Fiume and other ports.
	Bushels.		Bushels.	Bushels.	Bushels.	Bushels.	Bushels.	Bushels.	Bushels.
1875	1,707,349	$1,068,460	296,015	922,638	6,712	191,564	27,774	14,905	247,741
1876	4,047,307	2,637,120	2,449,133	963,023	33,385	143,453	59,004	198,561	200,728
1877	9,528,725	5,961,810	7,318,969	779,429	265,358	371,004	157,861	399,487	236,617
1878	8,433,238	5,275,470	6,508,528	764,517	162,065	244,929	218,992	283,797	250,410
1879	5,168,532	2,291,490	3,431,904	586,804	542,639	205,398	100,173	105,937	195,641
1880	11,227,633	7,027,810	5,411,571	585,230	601,177	11,480	222,328	1,241,235	3,094,612
Average	6,685,464	4,043,693	4,236,025	766,940	278,550	194,638	131,022	373,991	704,292

X.—*Tabular statement showing the quantity and value of maize exported from Austria-Hungary, and to or through which countries, during the years 1875-'80.*

[Quantities given in bushels at the rate of 3.93 bushels per metrical centner of 100 kilograms.]

Countries to or through which exported.

Years.	Quantity.	Value.	Germany.	Italy.	Servia and Turkey.	Other countries.	Trieste.	Fiume.
	Bushels.		Bushels.	Bushels.	Bushels.	Bushels.	Bushels.	Bushels.
1875	5,005,849	$3,549,370	3,252,153	4,177	3,631	2,793	1,608,562	134,543
1876	5,154,395	3,494,430	4,971,096	17,331	149	4,300	96,937	63,082
1877	2,381,304	2,110,680	1,916,409	222,764	28,430	14,438	108,413	90,850
1878	1,472,539	1,381,700	777,079	136,540	50,261	18,105	262,375	228,170
1879	4,460,361	2,908,130	2,518,541	729,377	62,911	40,970	270,753	837,809
1880	2,045,024	1,760,130	1,287,826	249,504	242,733	74,788	92,371	137,802
Average	3,419,912	2,534,440	2,454,001	226,615	64,686	10,233	406,567	248,810

XI.—*Tabular statement showing the quantity and value of flour imported into Austria-Hungary, and from or through which countries, during the years 1875-'80.*

[Quantities given in tons of 1,000 kilograms per ton.]

Countries from or through which imported.

Years.	Quantity.	Value.	Germany.	Russia.	Roumania.	Italy.	Servia and Turkey.	Other countries.	Fiume and other ports.
	Tons.		Tons.	Tons.	Tons.	Tons.	Tons.	Tons.	Tons.
1875	48,809	$3,392,750	42,016	41	165	219	23	1,135	2,110
1876	45,636	3,385,370	40,134	108	58	159	70	1,875	3,232
1877	48,584	3,375,940	41,600	178	37	217	42	1,292	2,278
1878	48,493	3,199,640	44,242	698	328	106	15	786	3,318
1879	58,449	3,335,760	45,568	6,291	488	952	51	2,527	2,572
1880	80,847	4,541,570	36,001	16,066	664	1,148		7,165	19,903
Average	54,130	3,538,505	41,594	3,897	274	483	33	2,463	5,392

XII.—*Tabular statement showing the quantity and value of flour exported from Austria-Hungary, and to or through which countries, during the years 1875-'80.*

[Quantities given in tons of 1,000 kilograms per ton.]

Years.	Quantity.	Value.	Countries to or through which exported.							
			Germany.	Russia.	Roumania.	Italy.	Servia and Turkey.	Switzerland.	Trieste.	Fiume and other ports.
	Tons.		*Tons.*	*Tons.*	*Tons.*	*Tons.*	*Tons.*	*Tons.*	*Tons.*	*Tons.*
1875	×3,639	$7,529,240	33,875	1,470	152	234	862	83	23,515	23,448
1876	112,802	10,156,930	58,257	548	242	520	1,938	50	24,652	26,595
1877	163,087	16,034,280	76,204	973	559	554	1,211	87	60,784	22,715
1878	231,683	20,880,800	111,788	1,219	771	810	3,625	215	75,620	37,635
1879	245,231	19,582,010	120,736	2,612	2,112	1,102	4,334	208	45,826	68,301
1880	133,021	10,074,110	54,099	1,440	2,756	1,491	215	194	29,713	43,113
Average .	161,577	14,042,910	75,826	1,377	1,099	785	2,031	139	43,352	36,968

XIII.—*Tabular statement showing the quantity of grain and flour, other mill products included, exported from and imported into the Empire of Austria-Hungary during the decade 1871–1880.*

[Reported in tons of 1,000 kilograms each.]

Description.	1871.	1872.	1873.	1874.	1875.	1876.	1877.	1878.	1879.	1880.	Averages.
Wheat:											
Import	61,344	119,465	207,814	248,178	103,099	116,213	143,017	147,440	214,606	225,243	170,868
Export	279,994	57,303	38,510	68,843	100,511	119,990	372,596	362,343	340,362	201,746	198,210
Balance	218,450	62,102	169,304	179,335	2,588	3,677	227,578	214,903	145,756	123,495	27,343
Rye:											
Import	21,869	45,188	160,472	252,629	39,029	36,610	64,987	36,345	93,351	104,633	86,534
Export	136,046	39,759	26,765	50,991	74,487	71,300	47,670	44,252	74,767	64,218	65,029
Balance	114,177	5,448	133,707	201,668	45,458	34,750	17,317	13,093	18,744	40,415	23,505
Spelt, millet, buckwheat, maslin:											
Import	1,427	7,440	9,800	12,402	1,081	2,741	4,913	7,882	11,645	16,671	7,702
Export	5,169	3,337	2,154	3,107	5,866	6,899	4,439	3,207	10,244	8,784	5,321
Balance	3,742	4,103	7,646	10,295	4,785	4,138	474	4,675	1,398	7,887	2,381
Maize:											
Import	80,985	243,049	180,391	143,181	43,444	102,085	242,461	214,586	131,515	285,690	166,634
Export	23,769	2,222	2,668	28,735	127,375	131,155	60,593	37,469	113,495	52,037	57,952
Balance	57,216	240,867	177,723	114,446	83,931	28,170	181,868	177,117	16,020	233,653	108,681
Barley malt:											
Import	12,062	27,691	39,903	50,663	13,687	16,837	56,413	48,758	30,901	36,142	33,769
Export	160,913	113,604	168,689	170,324	215,767	222,967	306,330	229,682	277,939	289,062	231,672
Balance	148,251	87,443	128,756	119,661	202,080	206,130	311,917	280,934	247,038	252,920	188,308
Oats:											
Import	11,749	18,770	20,378	35,350	11,472	13,878	14,997	14,374	19,149	17,908	17,862
Export	26,364	60,776	101,110	125,946	68,439	98,803	93,050	100,321	104,147	71,105	83,866
Balance	74,615	42,006	80,732	88,587	56,967	84,925	78,053	75,947	84,998	53,197	66,004
Total grain:											
Import	190,236	461,643	618,788	743,441	201,812	289,354	528,788	489,387	521,063	786,286	484,102
Export	632,254	278,411	358,805	445,946	392,415	651,673	946,678	867,284	960,934	686,953	640,189
Balance	442,018	183,232	278,893	297,496	390,633	361,789	417,690	377,897	439,301	99,333	157,087

XIII.—*Tabular statement showing the quantity of grain and flour, other mill products included, &c.*—Continued.

Description.	1871.	1872.	1873.	1874.	1875.	1876.	1877.	1878.	1879.	1880.	Averages.
Flour and other mill products:											
Import	20,328	29,368	61,168	57,480	45,809	45,636	45,584	48,493	58,449	80,847	49,316
Export	147,499	70,853	42,797	60,055	83,640	112,803	160,086	231,685	245,232	131,141	128,779
Balance	127,171	41,485	18,371	5,575	37,831	67,167	117,202	183,192	186,783	52,294	79,462

GRAIN HARVESTS AND MARKETS OF AUSTRIA-HUNGARY.

REPORT BY CONSUL-GENERAL WEAVER, OF VIENNA.

The tenth session of the International Grain Exchange was opened in this city on the 6th instant with appropriate formalities.

Among the reports produced on that occasion was that of Moriz Leinkauf, sketching the grain harvests of Austria-Hungary for 1882, which I regard of sufficient interest to justify me in forwarding you a full translation thereof, as follows:

The Vienna Grain Exchange, observing the custom of former years, has based its calculations, concerning the crop, on the area given in official publications.

For the estimates of this year's crop of winter grain in Hungary the official data of the fall season of 1879 were taken, and for the summer grain, those of the spring of 1880.

For the estimates of the crop in Austria, the data of the fall of 1880, and, respectively, the spring of 1881 were consulted.

In estimating the crops of Hungary, those areas were taken into consideration which, under ordinary circumstances, either on account of inundation or too great humidity, are left uncultivated.

The wheat crop of Hungary, as to quantity, is excellent; as to quality, for the greater part, very good, such as it has not been since 1867.

The surplus in Hungary is estimated by the experts of the Vienna Grain Exchange at twelve million hectoliters in excess of a full average crop.

In Austria, likewise, wheat in quantity will be above the average.

Lower Austria, Styria, Carinthia, Istria, Bohemia, Moravia, Silesia, Galicia, and Bukowina, in point of quantity, have wheat crops above the average, while the other provinces, for the greater part, show deficits. The quality of wheat in Hungary is also better than that of Austria. In Austria the farmers complain principally of sprouting, which in some parts has almost entirely destroyed the crops. This took place mostly in Upper Austria, Salzburg, Bohemia, and Moravia, where comparatively large quantities were rendered entirely unfit for human food. This was the case also in Western and Eastern Galicia, but to a less extent.

Our reports of the rye crop of Hungary are less satisfactory. Hungary cultivates about 1,100,000 hectares of summer rye, winter rye, and maslin. Our experts estimate that the crop will yield a surplus of 1,250,000 hectoliters over a full average crop. A similar proportion exists in Austria, where deficits in parts of Upper Austria, Bohemia, Moravia, Eastern Galicia, and Istria, are balanced by surplus and full average, and where, after all deductions are made, there will still be a surplus of 1,000,000 hectoliters. Despite all these circumstances the total monarchy will have a surplus of 2,250,000 hectoliters above the full average.

Concerning the summer grain, importance must be attached to the fact that large tracts of land, estimated at from 5 to 30 per cent. of the soil under cultivation in the single counties, could be planted during the year with barley, oats, and Indian corn, whereas this soil in other years was unproductive on account of inundation or too great humidity.

In barley, the surplus in Hungary is estimated at 2,500,000 hectoliters. The districts of Hungary which produce barley for brewing report average crops, while the districts cultivating barley for fodder report more abundant crops.

In Austria the barley crop is less favorable than in Hungary, and parts of Upper and Lower Austria, Bohemia, Moravia, and Istria, even show figures below an average.

The surplus in other districts, however, not only outbalances these shortcomings, but experts even estimate for Austria a surplus of nearly 1,000,000 hectoliters above the full average, giving for the whole monarchy 3,500,000 hectoliters barley above the full average. The quality, however, especially in Austria, leaves much to be desired.

The oat crop in both parts of the empire in point of quantity is very good. The total for Hungary is estimated to be more than 2,000,000 hectoliters above a full average.

In Austria, the following provinces have had bad crops: Upper and Lower Austria, Salzburg, Istria, and parts of Moravia, and Galicia. The greater part of oat-producing lands, however, shows such a considerable surplus, that 1,750,000 hectoliters above the full average may be relied on, and that the entire monarchy will have 4,000,000 hectoliters surplus above the full average crop.

Under ordinary circumstances the monarchy will, therefore, be able to export wheat (including flour) 13,000,000 to 14,000,000 metrical centners; rye, 2,000,000 to 2,500,000 metrical centners; barley for brewing, 3,000,000 to 3,500,000 metrical centners; barley for fodder, 2,000,000 metrical centners, and oats, 2,000,000 to 2,500,000 metrical centners.

The export will depend, of course, to some extent upon the crop of potatoes, legumes, and Indian corn. Potatoes and legumes have been injured by the heavy rains, and great fears were entertained concerning them, although, as regards the former, a fair crop may yet be realized, contingent upon better weather. Indian corn gives rise to the best hopes, and if the fall should be favorable for ripening the corn, the crop, especially in Hungary, will be an excellent one.

Taking the official statistics of crops which have been published in Hungary from 1869 to 1880 as a basis for calculation, the twelve years' average shows an annual product of about 21,000,000 hectoliters wheat, 15,000,000 hectoliters rye, 12,000,000 hectoliters barley, and 14,000,000 hectoliters oats.

In Austria the official statistics published show an average from 1870 to 1880 of 13,000,000 hectoliters wheat, 28,000,000 hectoliters rye, 16,000,000 hectoliters barley, 31,000,000 hectoliters oats.

Calling an average crop, therefore, 100, this year's crop in per cents. would be, in Hungary, wheat, 157; rye, 108½; barley, 120½; and oats, 116; and in Austria, wheat, 111½; rye, 103½; barley, 106; and oats, 105½.

In connection with the International Exchange the following valuable and interesting table was presented, showing the grain crops of Europe in 1882, estimating the average at 100:

Countries.	Wheat.	Rye.	Barley.	Oats.
Hungary	157	108½	120½	116
Italy:				
Upper	135	80		90
Central	110			
Southern	110			
France	100	90	100	110
Holland	105	105	105	10
Belgium	100	115	90	10
Great Britain and Ireland	100		110	15
Russia:				
Estland	145	145	85	900
Courland	95	95	85	180
Other northern parts	95	100	85	855
Podolia	115	100	80	80
Central	90	60	85	85
Southern, winter	95	90	195	100
summer	90			
Bessarabia	130	100	120	115
Russian Poland	120	130	95	
Roumania:				
Little Wallachia	120	130	100	
Great Wallachia	95	105	120	95
Moldavia	135	90	90	125
Servia	160	135	160	140

CEREALS OF GREECE.

REPORT BY CONSUL HANCOCK, OF PATRAS.

I have the honor to acknowledge receipt of your circular dispatch of the 31st May last requesting statistics for the past ten years respecting wheat, rye, and maize.

I regret to say that I am unable to give the information required, no account being kept here of the area planted or the quantity produced. This country does not export grain of any description; on the contrary, it imports both wheat and maize from Turkey and Russia, roughly speaking, half the yearly consumption. This year, however, the crops have been particularly favored, and the produce will reach fully two-thirds of the quantity required.

E. HANCOCK,
Consul.

UNITED STATES CONSULATE,
Patras, July 6, 1880.

GRAIN PRODUCTION OF ROUMANIA.

REPORT BY CONSUL-GENERAL SCHUYLER, OF BUCHAREST, ON THE PRODUCTION AND COMMERCE OF GRAIN IN ROUMANIA.

Owing to defects in Roumanian statistics it is impossible for me to answer with fullness and accuracy the questions contained in the circular of the Department dated May 31, 1882, with regard to statistics of the production of grain in Roumania for the last ten years. Statistics can be obtained only for the years 1876, 1877, 1879, and 1880. Those for 1878, owing to the war, were never made up.

1. The areas under the various cereal crops are not accurately known,

and no account is taken of changes from year to year. It was estimated that in 1881 the cultivated land in the kingdom was divided as follows:

	Acres.
Maize	4,423,800
Wheat	2,717,420
Barley	2,325,055
Rye	368,520
Oats	297,630
Buckwheat	30,230
Millet and small grains	278,000
Coltza	202,000
Hemp	42,000
Flax	23,000

2. The average annual production of Roumania is estimated as follows:

	Bushels.
Maize	43,000,000
Wheat	25,000,000
Barley	26,000,000
Rye	3,500,000
Oats	5,000,000
Millet	2,000,000
Buckwheat	350,000
Coltza	1,000,000

3. The following tables will show the quantities and values of wheat, rye, and maize exported from Roumania and the countries to which exported for the years 1876, 1877, 1879, and 1880. The quantities for 1876 are given only approximately, but are probably nearly exact:

WHEAT EXPORTED.

Country	1876 Bushels	1876 Dollars	1877 Bushels	1877 Dollars	1879 Bushels	1879 Dollars	1880 Bushels	1880 Dollars
Austria-Hungary	2,878,043	806,306	3,040,335	2,855,205		3,366,823	4,839,739	4,704,227
Belgium	52,209	51,341				4,272		711,903
Bulgaria							732,429	608,098
England	1,002,712	909,181	461,064	448,144		1,160,190	3,711,665	3,472,925
France	2,807,336	2,816,030	250,611	259,549		1,202,718	2,470,091	
Germany	66,726	50,226				37,963	6,598	6,414
Greece							418,067	407,236
Holland	804,124	765,945	112,748	109,663		462,664	90,616	86,078
Italy	12,830	12,411	26,576	26,552		375,322	234,195	234,838
Russia	8,350	8,755	12,105	11,874		6	61,487	50,726
Servia	3,048,320	2,866,246	373,528	365,023			851	827
Turkey	2,738,304	2,564,296	1,064,035	975,022		4,293,711	2,081,011	2,094,733
Other states						5,114,514		
Total	13,470,174	12,881,737	5,292,002	5,151,932	16,665,407	16,218,212	14,647,649	14,389,100

RYE EXPORTED.

Country	1876 Bushels	1876 Dollars	1877 Bushels	1877 Dollars	1879 Bushels	1879 Dollars	1880 Bushels	1880 Dollars
Austria-Hungary	443,640	275,053	300,519	243,684		414,396	742,434	463,280
Belgium	167,955	106,866				613	27,677	15,270
Bulgaria	1,851,413	1,133,832	274,121	171,051		602,038	1,006,615	628,127
England	237,124	148,174				156,612	211,064	131,943
France	80,248	49,930	9,491	6,138		9	54,494	33,998
Germany							31,787	19,835
Holland							303,003	189,074
Italy	41,205	41,666	12,870	8,029		57,835	1,756	1,096
Russia	6,032	3,884				3,534		
Turkey	726,625	701,294	47,068	29,932		93,780	71,036	44,326
Other states	712,097	418,685	178,561	111,424		116,639		
Total	4,290,270	2,879,384	913,530	570,258	2,316,470	1,445,463	2,449,856	1,528,949

MAIZE EXPORTED.

Countries	1876 Bushels.	1876 Dollars.	1877 Bushels.	1877 Dollars.	1879 Bushels.	1879 Dollars.	1880 Bushels.	1880 Dollars.
Austria-Hungary	3,649,172	2,354,362	7,673,298	4,972,297		2,974,389	6,422,085	4,161,511
Belgium	27,351	18,000				44,565	321,129	206,092
Bulgaria								
England	5,200,440	3,786,692	1,234,148	799,728		4,136,989	5,223,091	3,301,043
France	3,808,000	1,843,719	1,014,021	657,085		908,469	1,005,434	651,514
Germany	116,102	72,770	31,955	20,707		221,854	2,304	1,493
Greece							363,108	255,294
Holland			12,245	7,934			34,264	22,203
Italy	146,284	100,340	33,616	21,781		911,742	417,144	270,309
Russia	20,936	15,435	3,781	2,450		210,987	281,470	182,303
Servia	225	150				33,024	204,298	171,365
Turkey	2,379,162	1,650,679	223,967	145,131		1,648,400	225,654	145,835
Other states	2,541,300	1,036,122	815,730	528,593		2,398,794		
Total	16,948,872	11,467,389	11,042,761	7,135,706	20,955,384	13,570,213	14,569,381	9,440,927

4. The following tables show the quantities and values of wheat, rye, and maize imported into Roumania, and the countries from which imported, during the years 1876, 1877, 1879, and 1880. The quantities for 1876 are given only approximately, but are probably nearly exact:

WHEAT IMPORTED.

Country.	1876. Bushels.	1876. Dollars.	1877. Bushels.	1877. Dollars.	1879. Bushels.	1879. Dollars.	1880. Bushels.	1880. Dollars.
Austria-Hungary ..	2,653	2,000	20,288	19,720	....	1,070	1,836	1,785
Belgium	72	70	......	......	......	8	......	......
Bulgaria	......	......	......	......	......	......	5,824	5,660
England	......	......	......	......	......	......	......	......
France	249	243	......	......	......	......	94	91
Germany	18	18	......	......	......	......	......	......
Greece	......	......	......	......	......	......	11	11
Holland	......	......	......	......	......	......	......	......
Italy	......	......	......	......	......	......	......	......
Russia	115,583	112,013	467,008	453,931	......	30,974	16,038	15,588
Serbia	......	......	15,001	14,581	......	......	182	176
Turkey	1,030	1,010	195	189	......	7,303	......	......
Other states	7	7	......	......	......	1,053	......	......
Total	119,011	115,361	402,492	488,421	41,374	40,408	23,985	23,311

RYE IMPORTED.

Country.	1876. Bushels.	1876. Dollars.	1877. Bushels.	1877. Dollars.	1879. Bushels.	1879. Dollars.	1880. Bushels.	1880. Dollars.
Austria-Hungary ..	1,501	937	10,248	6,394	....	63	374	233
Belgium	......	......	......	......	......	......	......	......
Bulgaria	......	......	......	......	......	......	173	108
England	......	......	......	......	......	......	......	......
France	......	......	......	......	......	......	......	......
Germany	19	12	......	......	......	......	......	......
Greece	......	......	......	......	......	......	......	......
Holland	......	......	......	......	......	......	......	......
Italy	......	......	......	......	......	......	......	......
Russia	17,455	10,891	37,987	23,704	......	4,437	5,375	3,479
Serbia	......	......	......	......	......	......	......	......
Turkey	160	106	141	88	......	2	......	......
Other states	......	......	......	......	......	1,680	......	......
Total	19,144	11,946	48,376	30,186	9,909	6,182	6,122	3,820

MAIZE IMPORTED.

Country.	1876. Bushels.	1876. Dollars.	1877. Bushels.	1877. Dollars.	1879. Bushels.	1879. Dollars.	1880. Bushels.	1880. Dollars.
Austria-Hungary ..	27,083	17,549	27,868	18,057	....	3,723	21,524	13,948
Belgium	......	......	......	......	......	......	......	......
Bulgaria	......	......	......	......	......	......	214	199
England	......	......	......	......	......	......	18	12
France	......	......	......	......	......	......	......	......
Germany	......	......	......	......	......	......	......	......
Greece	......	......	......	......	......	......	......	......
Holland	......	......	......	......	......	......	......	......
Italy	......	......	......	......	......	......	......	......
Russia	14,153	9,180	284,610	184,427	......	7,087	20,008	12,965
Serbia	8	5	215	139	......	29	......	......
Turkey	14,460	9,371	126	81	......	8,806	12	7
Other states	151	116	9	6	......	11	......	......
Total	55,855	36,221	312,826	202,710	12,604	19,659	41,776	27,131

The following table will show the values of the grain exported for the years 1871 to 1880, inclusive:

Year.		Exports of—			
	Wheat.	Rye.	Maize.	Wheat flour.	Other flour.
1871	$13,779,445	$1,798,478	$8,066,530	$98,920	$2,663
1872	11,433,322	1,108,195	7,859,267	256,189	2,209
1873	9,377,958	339,803	6,811,125	148,470	5,622
1874	9,399,080	607,068	4,711,137	139,667	28,970
1875	13,622,369	489,776	4,894,882	200,132	3,542
1876	12,881,737	2,879,384	11,467,399	315,919	5,372
1877	5,151,932	570,258	7,155,706	388,418	48,862
1878	10,737,506	743,278	11,529,413	1,140,062	29,402
1879	16,218,215	1,445,453	13,579,218	647,605	15,646
1880	14,389,109	1,520,949	9,440,972	598,290	28,908

For the complete understanding of the grain trade of Roumania, I add tables showing the importation and exportation of wheat, rye, and maize flour during the years already mentioned. The quantities for 1876 are only given approximately, but are probably nearly exact.

WHEAT FLOUR EXPORTED.

Country.	1876.		1877		1879.		1880.	
	Pounds.	Dollars.	Pounds.	Dollars.	Pounds.	Dollars.	Pounds.	Dollars.
Austria-Hungary	210,534	5,186	32,689	801	....	22,212	2,040,649	55,899
Belgium	....	....	....	....	....	54	....	....
Bulgaria	....	....	....	....	....	....	2,416,279	65,898
England	558,800	16,572	....	....	....	225	....	....
France	24,420	8,140	....	....	....	6,012	....	....
Germany	....	....	....	....	....	....	....	....
Greece	....	....	....	....	....	....	218,387	5,956
Holland	....	....	....	....	....	....	....	....
Italy	....	....	....	....	....	....	....	....
Russia	....	263	3,223	88	....	14,588	1,421,250	38,761
Serbia	8,703	1,541	180,668	4,927	....	3,307	263,606	7,189
Turkey	56,532	282,729	14,014,451	382,512	....	573,231	15,568,190	424,587
Other states	10,553,157	1,488	....	....	....	27,976	....	....
Total	11,429,638	315,919	14,231,031	388,418	*23,750,003	647,605	21,937,361	598,290

RYE FLOUR EXPORTED.

Country.	1876.		1877		1879.		1880.	
Austria-Hungary	(*)	(*)	286	4	(*)	(*)	3,828	59
Belgium	....	....	....	....	....	....	....	....
Bulgaria	....	....	....	....	....	....	....	....
England	....	....	....	....	....	....	....	....
France	....	....	....	....	....	....	....	....
Germany	....	....	....	....	....	....	....	....
Greece	....	....	....	....	....	....	....	....
Holland	....	....	....	....	....	....	....	....
Italy	....	....	....	....	....	....	....	....
Russia	....	....	51,480	795	....	....	....	....
Serbia	....	....	....	....	....	....	....	....
Turkey	....	....	2,519,750	38,911	....	....	....	....
Other states	....	....	....	....	....	....	....	....
Total	....	....	2,571,516	39,710	....	....	3,828	59

* No statistics for 1876 and 1879.

MAIZE FLOUR EXPORTED.

Country.	1876.		1877.		1879,		1880.	
	Pounds.	Dollars.	Pounds.	Dollars.	Pounds.	Dollars.	Pounds.	Dollars.
Austria-Hungary	23,030	346	2,948	40	(*)	(*)	719,941	9,817
Belgium								
Bulgaria							156,123	2,129
England								
France								
Germany								
Greece							19,289	263
Holland								
Italy								
Russia	138,443	2,130					32,670	443
Serbia			499	6			43,065	587
Turkey	90,937	1,801	369,888	5,045			725,252	9,869
Other states								
Total	252,446	4,286	373,335	5,091			1,696,340	23,130

WHEAT FLOUR IMPORTED.

Country.	1876.		1877.		1879,		1880.	
	Pounds.	Dollars.	Pounds.	Dollars.	Pounds.	Dollars.	Pounds.	Dollars.
Austria-Hungary	1,222,342	36,710	2,148,579	58,597		167,675	7,804,504	212,850
Belgium								
Bulgaria							886,457	24,176
England						346	41	1
France	2,832	354				475	90,756	2,475
Germany						020	970	26
Greece							462	12
Holland								
Italy						15	2,442	66
Russia	120,502	3,243	1,905,072	51,956		11,643	262,378	7,155
Serbia			1,540	42		149	880	24
Turkey	2,277	87	1,845	50		47,618	73,850	2,215
Other states	1,734,367	47,308	1,892	38		123,726		
Total	3,082,720	87,702	4,058,428	110,683	12,916,585	352,267	9,122,740	249,000

RYE FLOUR IMPORTED.

Country.	1876.		1877.		1879,		1880.	
	Pounds.	Dollars.	Pounds.	Dollars.	Pounds.	Dollars.	Pounds.	Dollars.
Austria-Hungary	(*)	(*)	207,532	1,320	(*)	(*)	7,454	1,150
Belgium								
Bulgaria								
England								
France						●		
Germany								
Greece								
Holland								
Italy								
Russia			14,363,804	221,986			558	8
Serbia								
Turkey							20,178	312
Other states								
Total			14,571,336	223,306			95,190	1,470

* No statistics for 1876 and 1879.

MAIZE FLOUR IMPORTED.

Country.	1876.		1877.		1879,		1880.	
	Pounds.	Dollars.	Pounds.	Dollars.	Pounds.	Dollars.	Pounds.	Dollars.
Austria-Hungary	(*)	(*)	572	7	(*)	(*)	148,284	2,022
Belgium								
Bulgaria							29,990	400
England								
France								
Germany								
Greece								
Holland								
Italy			258,442	5,024			5,607	78
Serbia								
Turkey							18,002	245
Other states								
Total			259,014	5,031			201,883	2,754

* No statistics for 1876 and 1879.

It is to be remarked that the countries mentioned in all the preceding tables show merely the last place from which the grain was imported, or the primary destination of the exports, and proves nothing with regard to the origin of the grain or its ultimate destination.

There are export duties on grain in Roumania as follows: On wheat, 20 centimes per 100 kilograms (4 cents per 220 pounds); on rye, maize, barley, oats, millet, and buckwheat, 10 centimes per 100 kilograms (2 cents per 220 pounds). During the year 1880 the product of these duties amounted to $503,236.

By a law passed during the last year import duties have been placed on flour as follows: Wheat flour of every quality, 3.50 francs per 100 kilograms (67½ cents per 220 pounds); rye flour, 3 francs per 100 kilograms (58 cents per 220 pounds); maize, barley, millet, and buckwheat flour, 2 francs per 100 kilograms (38½ cents per 220 pounds); and on bran of every kind, 1 franc per 100 kilograms (19½ cents per 220 pounds).

EUGENE SCHUYLER,
Consul-General.

UNITED STATES CONSULATE-GENERAL,
Bucharest, September 13, 1883.

RUSSIAN CEREALS.

REPORT BY CONSUL-GENERAL STANTON, OF ST. PETERSBURG.

In reply to Department circular of May 31, 1882, I find myself nearly unable to give the information in the form desired. In this instance, also, application to the government was of little practical value.

The acreage under cultivation is not known, and is given in inclosure note as near as the authorities can guess at it in the absence of reliable statistical data.

The yield of maize cannot be ascertained from 1873, that grain having been incorporated with other cereals.

In reducing the rouble value to dollars, I have taken the average value of the rouble for the last two years, it being nearly impossible to ascertain the correct value, so great has been the fluctuation during the last ten years.

EDGAR STANTON,
Consul-General.

UNITED STATES CONSULATE-GENERAL,
St. Petersburg, September 2, 1882.

I.—AREA OF LAND UNDER CEREALS IN RUSSIA.

The area of land cultivated with cereals can only be approximately ascertained, no definite statistics existing on the subject. According to the estimates of a government commission appointed to investigate the condition of agriculture in Russia, which estimates are based upon the accounts of seed sown (87 bushels to 2.7 acres), there are annually under cultivation in European Russia (Poland excepted) the following areas, viz:

Area in acres according to the estimates of government commission and Mr. M. S. Yermoloff.

Wheat:	Estimates by commission.		Mr. Yermoloff's estimates.
Winter	6,126,300		7,749,000
Summer	20,764,890		20,871,000
		26,891,190	28,620,000
Rye	64,963,080		69,606,000
Oats	32,382,450		34,360,000
Barley	12,201,300		15,325,000
Buckwheat	11,318,400		11,367,000
Other cereals	10,530,000		
Cultivated land	158,286,420		
Uncultivated	80,214,300		
Total acres	238,500,720		

II.—*Yield of various cereals, reduced to bushels.*

Russia and Poland, exclusive of Don Cossack districts.	1870.	1871.	1872.	1873.
Wheat	214,141,800	178,785,000	153,340,400	157,562,800
Rye	609,752,000	579,588,200	549,248,400	614,231,600
Oats	586,235,000	396,847,600	545,356,600	464,626,400
Barley	127,368,000	108,999,400	123,679,200	
Buckwheat	103,267,000	62,286,200	86,541,800	
Other cereals	96,396,000	1,394,556,400	76,386,000	281,584,200
Total	1,737,192,800	1,394,557,800	1,534,552,400	1,518,005,000

	1874.	1875.	1876.	1877.	1878.
Wheat	249,197,000	145,875,800	154,268,400	246,285,400	293,702,600
Rye	700,100,600	544,115,400	528,078,600	626,243,400	709,583,600
Oats	467,503,200	397,636,400	512,256,000	492,437,400	537,625,200
Other cereals	270,918,000	234,412,800	305,735,400	312,202,400	301,118,600
Total	1,687,718,800	1,322,040,400	1,500,332,400	1,677,168,600	1,742,030,000

III.—*Quantities and values of exports across the frontier.*

Date.	Wheat.	Rye.	Maize.
1871:			
Bushels	66,816,000	22,620,000	
1872:			
Bushels	57,101,000	13,834,000	
1873:			
Bushels	40,368,000	42,862,000	3,828,000
Roubles	80,407,958	49,348,467	4,179,414
Dollars	40,203,979	24,674,234	2,080,707
1874:			
Bushels	57,096,000	56,318,000	754,000
Roubles	85,854,588	74,577,856	961,770
Dollars	42,927,294	37,288,928	480,885
1875:			
Bushels	55,274,000	33,118,000	684,000
Roubles	99,267,013	40,141,535	810,433
Dollars	119,633,507	20,070,768	405,217
1876:			
Bushels	53,571,798	46,814,309	2,185,440
Roubles	101,789,818	57,208,150	1,766,108
Dollars	50,897,909	28,604,075	883,054
1877:			
Bushels	50,217,913	57,984,897	2,911,948
Roubles	104,431,862	84,029,697	2,747,582
Dollars	52,215,931	42,014,849	1,373,791

III.—*Quantities and values of exports across the frontier*—Continued.

Date.	Wheat.	Rye.	Maize.
1878:			
Bushels	100, 142, 472	58, 063, 772	5, 790, 213
Roubles	204, 483, 165	76, 228, 011	4, 215, 508
Dollars	102, 241, 583	38, 114, 005	2, 107, 754
1879:			
Bushels	80, 736, 000	69, 716, 000	8, 990, 000
Roubles	185, 760, 000	96, 250, 000	7, 800, 000
Dollars	92, 880, 000	48, 125, 000	3, 900, 000
1880:			
Bushels	35, 607, 917	34, 611, 172	8, 218, 935
Roubles	80, 059, 059	65, 192, 406	10, 304, 327
Dollars	44, 529, 530	32, 596, 203	5, 152, 164

IV.—*Exports across the European frontier.*

Whither.	1876.	1877.	1878.	1880.
	Bushels.	*Bushels.*	*Bushels.*	*Bushels.*
Great Britain:				
Wheat	21, 869, 528	10, 850, 114	33, 810, 381	11, 767, 819
Rye	6, 200, 535	3, 455, 579	8, 773, 163	3, 846, 078
Maize	1, 458, 397	478, 283	3, 058, 789	2, 703, 430
Germany:				
Wheat	5, 711, 305	13, 817, 960	14, 902, 088	3, 915, 005
Rye	25, 232, 650	32, 435, 473	25, 176, 344	15, 808, 904
Maize	847	1, 011	22, 751	1, 745
France:				
Wheat	10, 517, 642	2, 565, 385	26, 465, 465	8, 949, 827
Rye	199, 8n8	192, 885	187, 751	243, 494
Maize	251, 276	110, 245	874, 988	506, 533
Austria:				
Wheat	4, 928, 585	8, 358, 130	7, 260, 876	3, 929, 762
Rye	3, 360, 214	3, 544, 536	7, 845, 304	1, 070, 355
Maize	145, 963	1, 673, 488	857, 806	1, 622, 749
Holland:				
Wheat	2, 420, 643	2, 141, 637	3, 356, 248	596, 505
Rye	4, 646, 859	7, 869, 470	5, 651, 931	4, 991, 515
Norway and Sweden:				
Wheat	261, 411	172, 933	111, 557	....
Rye	3, 320, 167	7, 127, 055	6, 832, 284	3, 988, 748
Maize			11, 204	
Denmark:				
Wheat	297, 411	635, 027	549, 502	36, 420
Rye	2, 008, 459	1, 703, 750	1, 183, 356	1, 358, 776
Belgium:				
Wheat	2, 043, 643	876, 406	1, 523, 148	1, 150, 798
Rye	1, 240, 983	1, 555, 575	2, 048, 517	1, 062, 565
Maize		7, 545	163, 618	59, 170
Portugal:				
Wheat	....	....	12, 331	....
Italy:				
Wheat	3, 086, 392	853, 538	6, 846, 219	2, 872
Rye	103, 260	....	205, 959	1, 920, 221
Maize	9, 544	701	137, 354	232
Spain:				
Wheat	19, 720	....	407, 218	131, 236
Turkey:				
Wheat	1, 220, 469	368, 820	2, 556, 800	....
Rye	9, 953	29, 000	80, 723	1, 224, 380
Maize	43, 497	90, 954	144, 334	1, 159, 256
Roumania:				
Wheat	254, 277	340, 374	1, 112, 122	1, 216, 555
Rye	19, 556	59, 939	46, 927	1, 375, 997
Maize	275, 916	539, 861	521, 300	78, 287
Greece:				
Wheat	625, 333	239, 430	1, 182, 207	1, 042, 465
Rye	....	....	30, 513	741, 134
Maize	....	9, 860	....	....
Other lands:				
Wheat	315, 439	....	31, 320	35, 052
Rye	1, 165, 785	11, 615	....	....
Total: Wheat	53, 571, 798	50, 217, 913	100, 142, 472	35, 607, 917
Rye	46, 814, 309	57, 984, 897	58, 063, 772	33, 611, 172
Maize	2, 185, 440	2, 911, 948	5, 790, 213	8, 218, 935

Exports across the Asiatic frontier.

Whither.	1876.	1877.	1878.	1880.
Total: { Wheat	53,592,045	50,218,899	100,153,602	35,622,927
Rye	46,814,599	57,984,897	58,072,002	35,611,172
Maize	2,792,908	2,983,050	6,535,594	8,218,935

V.—Grain imports across European frontier, in pounds.

From—	1876.	1877.	1878.	1880.
Sweden and Norway:	Pounds.	Pounds.	Pounds.	Pounds.
Wheat, pease, and beans	1,296			
Rye, barley, and maize	395,424			176,112
Germany:				
Wheat, pease, and beans	6,260,436	545,366	3,335,148	991,836
Rye, barley, and maize	6,690,420	1,869,012	3,684,528	11,563,056
Denmark:				
Wheat, pease, and beans				945,900
Rye, barley, and maize				178,884
Holland:				
Wheat, pease, and beans	2,340			648,000
Austria:				
Wheat, pease, and beans	717,084	114,732	215,856	972
Rye, barley, and maize	512,352	75,924	200,352	1,945,188
Turkey:				
Wheat, pease, and beans	23,724			
Rye, barley, and maize	14,760			113,400
Roumania:				
Wheat, pease, and beans	2,132,964	22,608	5,959,908	3,625,956
Rye, barley, and maize	1,948,572	2,921,112	2,661,768	20,185,020
France:				
Wheat, pease, and beans		432		1,908
Rye, barley, and maize	7,502			
Great Britain:				
Wheat, pease, and beans			180	17,264
Rye, barley, and maize	4,932		144	2,714,832
Belgium:				
Wheat, pease, and beans				664,200
United States:				
Wheat, &c.				1,025,040
Other lands:				
Wheat, pease, and beans	7,200			
Rye, barley, and maize				
Total: { Wheat, pease, and beans	9,137,844	673,088	9,511,092	7,991,676
Rye, barley, and maize	9,575,172	4,866,048	6,606,792	36,876,492

Grain imports across Asiatic frontier.

	1876	1877	1878	1880
Turkey: All cereals except rice	20,757,348	110,628	141,156	676,980
Persia: All cereals except rice	9,303,782	6,791,040	2,368,980	12,180,060
France: All cereals except rice				198,252
Total	30,061,080	6,901,668	2,510,136	13,055,292

CEREAL PRODUCTION OF TURKEY.

TWO REPORTS BY CONSUL-GENERAL HEAP, OF CONSTANTINOPLE.

FIRST REPORT.

I have delayed my report in answer to your circular, dated 31st May last, requiring statistics relative to the cereal production and commerce of the Ottoman Empire, in the hope that I might be able to obtain from some source the information required. I have written in every direction, both officially and unofficially, to ask for data which might enable me to give at least an approximate estimate of the produce of cereals, the acreage under cultivation, and the export and import of grain, &c., of Turkey. Reports have been made to me which, although probably correct enough in some respects, were generally so vague and incomplete, and covered such limited areas, or were from such small districts, as to be quite valueless in the absence of general statistics from entire provinces or principal divisions of the empire.

From Anatolia I am informed that the breadstuffs raised are wheat, barley, maize, and millet—rye not being cultivated in that province; but here accuracy ends, for I am told that the areas of these crops are this year as follows:

Acres.

Wheat	444,444
Barley	333,333
Maize	244,444
Millet	177,777

I am also informed that when crops are good an acre will yield from 34 to 48 bushels of wheat or other cereal. '

With more apparent correctness it is stated that from 1872 to 1876 the crops of cereals hardly sufficed for the supply of the local demand, and no shipments were made during these years except in small quantities to the islands of the Archipelago, the price of wheat ranging from $1.22 to $1.44 per bushel, according to quality. In 1877 the destruction caused by locusts nearly created a famine, which continued up to 1881. The crops fell short for local use during these years, and breadstuffs were imported.

In 1881, 364,000 bushels of barley were exported to England, France, Spain, and Portugal, at 75 cents to $1.10 per bushel.

In 1879 and 1880 the prices of breadstuffs were very high, and wheat, barley, and maize were imported in large quantities from Egypt, Syria, Roumania, and Roumelia.

The yearly importations during those years at Smyrna, the principal port of the province of Anatolia, or vilayet of Aidin, were 728,000 and 910,000 bushels of wheat, at $1.53 to $2.34 per bushel; 369,000 bushels of maize, at $1 to $1.53 per bushel, and 180,000 bushels of barley, at 81 cents to $1.16 per bushel.

Odessa, Galatz, Braila, Constantinople, Alexandria, and Marseilles supplied Smyrna during those two years with about 180,000 sacks of flour, weighing on an average 198 pounds, at about $6 per sack.

Smyrna imported in 1879 about 1,000 quarters of American maize (white and spotted) which was found to be of very good quality. It came by way of Liverpool and Marseilles. The white sold at $1.23 per bushel and the spotted at $1.11 per bushel.

In 1879 and 1880 about 1,000 barrels of American flour were imported, but were sold with difficulty, owing to its superior quality and high price. It sold at from 3 cents to 4½ cents per pound.

The imports from abroad were large, as several places in the interior, outside the vilayet of Aidin, draw their supplies from Smyrna.

These statistics were furnished by Mr. Griffith, the vice and deputy consul at Smyrna; but he expresses a doubt as to their being reliable, and he, like all my other correspondents, complains of the total absence of trustworthy data.

Since the financial administration has been placed in the hands of foreigners, principally Germans, pains will perhaps be taken to collect statistics which will show how little is really known of the internal resources of this country. The almost entire absence of roads or means of economical transportation has, as one of its consequences, the effect of discouraging cultivation in districts at a distance from the seaboard. It is sometimes seen that whilst in one province the scarcity of cereals is so great as to render it necessary, in the view of the government, to prohibit their exportation, in a neighboring one the harvests are so abundant as to leave a large surplus, but which, for want of economical transportation, cannot be conveyed without loss to supply the wants of the district where scarcity prevails

In compliance with my request, the consular agent at Salonica convened a special commission, composed of some of the first merchants of the place and landed proprietors of the provinces to prepare a report on the produce of Macedonia, one of the richest provinces of European Turkey, but they found at their first meeting that they could do nothing in consequence of the want of the most elementary statistics. He says that he might be able to give an approximate estimate of the harvests of this and last year, but that it is quite impossible to state the area under cultivation, and, of course, equally difficult to state that of the last ten years.

Mr. Calvert, the consular agent at the Dardanelles, writes :

I have done my best to obtain the information you request in your official dispatch, but regret to say have made but indifferent progress. The Turks are not a statistical people, and their method of conducting public business is against recapitulation. The tithes of the province up to the last few years were farmed out to fifty different persons, who again sub-farmed. At the department I was promised information, but have been put off from week to week. I can place no dependence on receiving it. The value of grain for several years past I can give, and the average yield per acre. As to the quantities exported and imported, the custom-house authorities are reluctant to furnish.

The public offices are unable to aid us in any way in arriving at the information we require. As regards the custom-house records it is notorious that exporters underestimate the amounts they export in order to reduce the tax, and in the case of sailing vessels their destination is not mentioned, as they generally call at another port for orders.

In the course of my inquiries I have ascertained that other governments have repeatedly instructed their agents in Turkey to furnish them with similar information, and that their efforts have obtained no better results than mine.

The commercial report I made in 1881, and which was published in August of that year, has served as the basis for several reports made from here, and even the Turks have used it as a source from which to draw when asked for information. As no high degree of accuracy or completeness can be claimed for it, but only that it was made from the best materials available, this fact will show how little they can rely upon their own records if they have to trust to the report of a foreign consul for information regarding their internal resources and productions.

With this explanation I beg to express my regret that, with every desire and after every effort to comply with your instructions, I have been unable to furnish such a report as would be in any degree accurate or serviceable. It is comparatively easy for consuls residing in countries where the public administrations are regulated by rules and order, to obtain printed statistics on every subject, bristling with facts and figures, but consuls in Turkey have no such facilities. Officials here are generally quite willing to give such information as they may have, but there is such want of system and so much disorder in their records that it is quite hopeless even with the best intentions to obtain from them a systematic statement of facts covering any lengthened period.

As an instance in point I will state that two years ago, having occasion to make application at one of the ministries of the Porte for a firman, and it being necessary to refer my application to the governor of the district covered by the firman, before it could be granted, several weeks were lost, because neither the minister nor any of his subordinates could discover in what vilayet the locality was situated.

G. H. HEAP,
Consul-General.

UNITED STATES CONSULATE-GENERAL,
Constantinople, August 31, 1882.

SECOND REPORT.

I venture to transmit further details, received since the date of my former report, relative to the cereal crops of Turkey, but as they are confined to the pachalic of Palestine, comprising only the districts of Jerusalem, Hebron, Gaza, and Jaffa, they are far from answering the wide scope of the circular of the Department, dated May 31, 1882, and I give them for what they may be worth, referring to my dispatch of the 31st August instant last for explanation of the causes which render it impossible to give the statistics that circular calls for.

The areas under cultivation of cereals in the four districts mentioned above have varied from 150,000 to 200,000 acres during the last ten years. This is the gross amount, for it has been found impossible to obtain, even approximately, the number of acres cultivated with each cereal.

In 1881 the tithes collected amounted to about £100,000 Turkish, or $430,000, but in view of the difficulty to obtain access to Turkish records, especially during the present political situation, this amount is stated as an estimate only.

The harvest of 1881 was a good one in cereals, and the price of wheat, barley, and maize fell to about one-half of what it was in 1879. The price of wheat per bushel was $1 of barley 50 cents, and of maize 75 cents.

The harvest this year is also a fair one, but prices are not stated at this time. A report from Mr. Hardegg, the United States consular agent at Jaffa, shows that the harvests of 1879 and 1880 were bad, and that very little grain was exported in 1879 and none at all in 1880.

This information is derived from Mr. Merrill, the United States consul at Jerusalem, and he has also sent me a report from Mr. Hardegg, of which I inclose a copy. It refers only to the rural district and port of Jaffa.

I regret that I am precluded by the lack of statistics and the inability if not unwillingness of those who should be able to impart some information, from giving more precise answers to the questions of the circular. When I have made inquiries of the authorities here they seemed surprised that I should imagine that such information existed in their records.

G. H. HEAP,
Consul-General.

UNITED STATES CONSULATE-GENERAL,
Constantinople, September 12, 1882.

Report of Consular Agent Hardegg, of Jaffa.

[Inclosure in Consul-General Heap's report.]

I regret not to be able to give you all the statistical information you desire for the consul-general at Constantinople, as indicated in your dispatch No. 5. With regard to questions 1 and 2, the respective Turkish officials, who might have possessed the needed information, emphatically refused to give me access to their archives, as the present political situation would not allow them to give any such information to any consul without a higher order from Constantinople. However, if a reliable estimate of the area of cultivated soil in this district will be acceptable to you, I will state that it has varied from 20,000 to 25,000 acres during the last eight years.

The amount of receipts from the tithes of last year was 15,000 Turkish pounds, or $64,500.

In answer to questions 3 and 4, I beg to submit to you the following tables, beginning with the year 1873, of exports:

Exports of cereals from Jaffa.

Articles.	Quantities.	Value.	Whither exported.
	Bushels.		
1873 :			
Barley	118,000	$90,000	} France and England.
Wheat	336,000	330,000	
1874 :			
Barley	126,000	114,200	} France, Austria, and England.
Maize	24,500	15,000	
Wheat	392,000	470,000	
1875 :			
Barley	100,000	75,000	} France, Egypt, and England.
Maize	20,000	10,000	
Wheat	955,000	650,000	
1876 :			
Barley	600,000	160,000	} England and France.
Maize	75,000	50,000	
Wheat	400,000	300,000	
1877 :			
Maize	55,000	22,000	} France.
Wheat	140,000	112,000	
1878 :			
Barley	11,000	6,000	} France and England.
Wheat	66,000	70,000	
1879 :			
Maize	20,000	12,000	France.
1880 :			
No exportations			
1881 :			
Barley	50,000	22,500	} France, England, and Egypt.
Maize	350,000	200,000	
Wheat	200,000	245,000	

Imports of cereals at Jaffa.

No imports from 1873 to 1878, both inclusive.

Articles.	Quantities.	Value.	Whence imported.
	Bushels.		
1879 :			
Barley	30,000	20,000	} From France and Egypt.
Wheat	70,000	90,000	
1880 :			
Barley	20,000	14,000	} From Egypt.
Maize	125,000	150,000	
Wheat	250,000	377,000	

E. HARDEGG,
Consular Agent.

UNITED STATES CONSULAR AGENCY,
Jaffa, August 9, 1882.

CEREALS OF INDIA.

REPORT BY CONSUL-GENERAL MATTSON, OF CALCUTTA.

In reply to the circular of the State Department dated May 31, 1882, asking for certain agricultural statistics, I have the honor to report that after collecting all the available information on the subject I find it quite impossible to furnish any reliable statistics in regard to the area, quantity, or yield of cereals in India for the last ten years, or for any single year thereof.

In a dispatch to this consulate under date the 9th September, the honorable the under secretary to the government of India, department of revenue and agriculture, says:

Hitherto no systematic arrangements have existed for recording such statistics, and it is not expected that they will, for some provinces, be obtainable in anything like complete form for some years.

Through the kind assistance of the honorable the assistant secretary to the government of India, department of finance and commerce, I am enabled to present the following complete tables, which are inclosed herewith:

A.—Statement showing the quantities and value of wheat imported into and exported from British India during the last ten years, whence imported and whither exported.

B.—Statement showing the quantities and value of wheat imported to and exported from British India by land in each year from 1877–'78 to 1881–'82, and the countries from which imported and to which exported.

Rye and maize are not exported from or imported to India, except that very small quantities may pass among the cereals denominated grain and pulse; hence no statistics are available.

Imports and exports of wheat by land can only be given for five years, as the trade was not registered before the year 1877–'78.

H. MATTSON,
Consul-General.

UNITED STATES CONSULATE-GENERAL,
Calcutta, October 3, 1882.

A.—Statement showing the quantities and value of wheat imported into and exported from British India by sea in each year from 1872-'73 to 1881-'82, and the countries from which imported and to which exported.

IMPORTS.

Quantities in bushels.

Countries from which imported.	1872-'73.	1873-'74.	1874-'75.	1875-'76.	1876-'77.	1877-'78.	1878-'79.	1879-'80.	1880-'81.	1881-'82.
Arabia	6,091	12,004		1,191	17,162	23,147	23,197	2		66,011
Persia			87,245	52	8,960	184,061	329,030	15,630		87,976
Turkey in Asia	76	1,370		34,031	85,949	597,495	412,606	7,474	30	232,269
Other countries			123	1,406	660	767	2,919	154	117	30
Total	6,167	13,374	87,358	36,680	112,731	805,476	767,752	23,260	153	386,286

EXPORTS.

Quantities in bushels.

Countries to which exported.	1872-'73.	1873-'74.	1874-'75.	1875-'76.	1876-'77.	1877-'78.	1878-'79.	1879-'80.	1880-'81.	1881-'82.
United Kingdom (or Great Britain)	371,039	2,535,105	745,718	3,876,785	6,096,122	10,698,518	1,597,273	3,037,022	8,964,188	17,507,907
Austria	7,216		47,591	11,144	3,860	1,663			6,348	59,052
Belgium					319,472	14,930		56,599	422,158	4,900,423
France		51,546	384,137	324,029	1,047,709	217,792	20,556	138,439	2,513,933	9,908,403
Holland						45,035		47,744	981,995	1,329,795
Italy		25,084	175,052	49,295	123,051	78,351			254,848	670,727
Malta		10,003	61,684	18,848	358,178	196,403			115,539	201,006
Egypt	30,550	99,219	62,442	180,087	78,014	48,733	92,684	75,562	67,583	1,715,534
Reunion	149,852	208,828	167,647	40,117	191,983	289,124	82,887	57,290	147,073	72,824
Mauritius	40,641	16,740	29,760	46,538	24,785	48,877	40,199	55,147	89,514	116,996
Aden	6,897	155,086	57,448	43,932	5,206	13,328	2,303	123,219	198,362	65,609
Arabia	40,009	84,461	46,182		41,701	50,385	31,843	21,033	24,025	181,899
Ceylon								381,119	204,114	109,485
Turkey in Asia						17	125		145,563	
Persia	15,735	625	541	174	80,644	54,146	38,925	52,983	38,597	665
Straits Settlements	60,334	67,659	69,119	55,457		77,644	43,346	36,387	21,746	25,009
Other countries	17,012	23,424	48,247	16,872	51,442			15,827		219,217
Total	736,485	3,277,780	1,995,608	4,663,278	10,422,227	11,834,946	1,950,123	4,098,360	13,896,166	37,078,570

A.—*Statement showing the quantities and values of wheat imported into and exported from British India, &c.*—Continued.

IMPORTS.

Value.

Countries from which imported.	1872-73.	1873-74.	1874-75.	1875-76.	1876-77.	1877-78.	1878-79.	1879-80.	1880-81.	1881-82.
Arabia				$997	$11,414	$30,307	$453,180	$43		$55,863
Persia	$4,648	$9,234	$46,178	42	6,675	171,337	326,420	15,110		76,904
Turkey in Asia		1,544		28,176	62,821	369,369	419,181	7,022	$38	190,822
Other countries	95		100	1,111	4,476	871	2,852	226	117	53
Total	4,743	10,788	66,278	30,326	85,386	762,044	771,703	22,361	155	323,702

EXPORTS.

Value.

Countries to which exported.	1872-73.	1873-74.	1874-75.	1875-76.	1876-77.	1877-78.	1878-79.	1879-80.	1880-81.	1881-82.
United Kingdom (or Great Britain)	$365,444	$2,574,260	$718,071	$2,936,107	$3,997,686	$10,283,289	$1,696,338	$3,218,504	$8,183,097	$15,862,372
Austria	2,029		35,180	11,948	4,724	1,560			6,083	48,556
Belgium					280,343	17,062		71,600	450,483	4,705,729
France		50,472	478,686	263,136	885,766	215,770	59,416	147,446	2,546,243	9,551,543
Holland									500,897	1,073,084
Italy		29,469	191,267	52,406	123,245	44,712		58,281	275,826	670,854
Malta		12,732	57,683	17,736	270,550	84,861			107,679	203,823
Egypt						169,000				1,543,152
Reunion	19,948	88,730	58,029	22,297	56,754	50,940	106,016	88,140	64,176	63,750
Mauritius	127,483	212,465	154,283	36,374	143,483	276,734	89,916	62,300	148,106	100,033
Aden	37,878	16,721	28,945	45,468	21,606	60,808	53,537	72,473	97,738	63,532
Arabia	7,416	160,673	60,332	4,518		13,870	2,734	146,970	207,474	182,953
Ceylon	42,440	83,369	41,481	38,377	42,466	67,364	48,196	32,190	28,964	97,022
Turkey in Asia						3				
Persia	12,941	590	550	191		17	132		223,498	
Straits Settlement	47,755	37,820	63,090	27,046	59,674	30,216	42,058	62,332	147,608	652
Other countries	17,466	22,104	56,143	31,747	39,320	82,055	53,751	39,435	33,946	20,361
								21,376	21,529	224,110
Total	670,700	3,310,425	1,961,740	3,644,102	7,825,330	11,427,539	2,055,114	4,484,059	13,111,766	34,416,326

B.—*Statement showing the quantities and values of wheat imported to and exported from British India by land in each year from 1877-78 to 1881-82, and the countries from which imported and to which exported.*

IMPORTS.

Countries from which imported.	Quantity in bushels.					Value.				
	1877-78.	1878-79.	1879-80.	1880-81.	1881-82.	1877-78.	1878-79.	1879-80.	1880-81.	1881-82.
Khelat	20,240	12,938	13,126	7,821	11,602	$18,472	$12,887	$13,118	$7,215	$9,892
Seestan	11,362	11,612	12,402	274	2,774	8,310	13,441	11,007	531	2,037
Kandahar	10,987	35	17			9,639	46	13		
Kabul	23,250	27,733	37,089	4,004	1,606	16,277	20,832	57,246	6,380	1,502
Bajaur	22,174	9,165	7,360	174	28	13,642	8,170	12,762	303	30
Kashmir	23,320	16,947	4,024	5,652	23,835	13,126	13,228	3,942	4,148	18,429
Nepal	28,836	32,545	45,442	129,713	94,075	26,468	26,607	37,981	81,057	54,325
Upper Burma	75,904	49,226	18,424	31,386	60,702	73,502	52,392	19,534	29,769	46,505
Other countries	2,477	1,087	838	123	842	3,854	971	892	176	738
Total	218,559	161,285	139,522	179,147	197,465	183,296	148,574	156,500	129,270	133,458

EXPORTS.

Countries to which exported.	Quantity in bushels.					Value.				
	1877-78.	1878-79.	1879-80.	1880-81.	1881-82.	1877-78.	1878-79.	1879-80.	1880-81.	1881-82.
Sewestan	14,999	22,030	7,147	12,561	6,399	$7,290	$15,503	$6,634	$13,712	$4,658
Kabul	26,522	16,600	27,181	27,233	25,304	14,023	10,806	36,253	31,675	21,897
Bajaur	10,360	9,136	4,902	1,015	1,162	6,091	7,023	6,302	1,343	1,005
Kashmir	282,529	175,601	100,556	65,347	33,695	213,463	102,234	150,828	45,630	17,836
Thibet	2,682	4,840	2,863	4,773	5,465	1,591	3,767	2,574	3,350	4,667
Other countries	3,606	12,271	1,409	5,186	2,796	2,561	9,616	1,563	6,467	2,583
Total	340,907	240,508	214,058	116,125	74,911	245,021	179,041	204,154	102,177	52,568

ALGERIA.

REPORT BY CONSUL JOURDAN, OF ALGIERS.

Statistics of cereals from 1871 to 1870.

Year	Cereals	Area planted.	Yield.	Exports.			Imports.		
		Acres.	*Bushels.*	Quantity.*Bushels.*	Whither.	Value.	Quantity.*Bushels.*	Whence imported.	Value.
1871	Wheat	1,963,126	9,055,898	1,469,363	France	$2,812,385	35,255	France and Spain	$56,492
	Barley	1,402,812	10,419,835	903,900	do	1,372,960	48,782	France, Spain, Italy, and Tunis	66,399
	Maize	38,425	224,155		do		5,674	France and Tunis	3,435
	Rye	5,877	17,215	9,375	do	11,372	376	France	146
	Oats	48,793	480,782	390,838	do	557,904	1,083	do	1,203
1872	Wheat	2,131,350	13,130,444	2,516,555	do	4,813,483	111,454	France, Russia, and Spain	107,703
	Barley	2,080,572	17,233,491	1,117,784	do	1,625,868	202,075	do	159,780
	Maize	54,352	370,774		do		7,768	France and Spain	4,716
	Rye	5,130	13,972		do		11	France	7
	Oats	47,265	603,612	327,349	do	607,083	1,201	France and Spain	1,080
1873	Wheat	2,378,757	14,574,765	3,152,808	do	6,926,825	38,758	France, Austria, and Spain	680,266
	Barley	684,707	17,406,268	2,660,616	do	5,604,452	59,102	France, Spain, Italy, and Turkey	11,249
	Maize	35,041	473,070	33	do	36	32,378	do	19,661
	Rye	2,357	18,857	914	do	877	13	France	12
	Oats	46,517	611,619	385,318	do	588,877	38	France and Russia	174
1874	Wheat	2,229,132	18,775,872	315,914	do	3,329,394	41,285	France, Russia, Spain, and India	72,664
	Barley	2,307,552	22,003,289	2,285,318	do	2,576,873	43,675	France, Spain, Italy	36,725
	Maize	49,327	372,466	110,143	do		11,308	France, Spain, Italy, and Turkey	6,890
	Rye	2,902	31,127	82	do	91		France	
	Oats	50,882	662,340	247,656	do	459,290	6,736	France, Spain, and Russia	6,701
1875	Wheat	3,329,800	17,148,723	1,946,532	do	3,713,185	9,405	France, Spain, Turkey, and Barbary	18,048
	Barley	3,720,692	32,191,491	1,677,148	do	2,267,736	14,451	France, Spain, Turkey, and Barbary	11,431
	Maize	50,765	136,466		do		18,029	France, Italy, and Turkey	11,914
	Rye	5,682	46,070	27	do	30	77	France	75
	Oats	53,177	637,390	316,493	do	587,188	950	France and Spain	1,886
1876	Wheat	3,302,926	14,732,737	2,980,041	do	5,719,113	135,302	France, Italy, Tunis, and Spain	121,127
	Barley	3,683,697	27,268,604	2,299,953	do	3,214,536	45,276	France and Tunis	32,480
	Maize	51,535	351,105		do		3	France	2
	Rye	5,517	29,368	27	do	30	449	do	364
	Oats	72,097	894,867	464,079	do	901,828	76,418	France and Spain	134,524
1877	Wheat	3,375,900	10,542,882	1,078,863	do	3,640,558	49,224	France, Turkey, and Tunis	42,158
	Barley	3,513,737	13,921,791	553,963	do	805,120	21,835	France, Italy, and Barbary	13,089
	Maize	56,546	213,647	11	do	12	165	do	141
	Rye	3,405	22,858		do			France	
	Oats	856,125	927,382	293,953	do	545,164			

CEREALS OF ALGERIA.

Year	Article							Exported to—	
1878	Wheat	3,009,207	12,625,272	537,668	do	1,028,466	444,854	France, Italy, and Tunis	971,922
	Barley	3,188,467	15,723,290	374,142	do	543,916	580,114	France, Russia, and Turkey	592,934
	Maize	82,687	218,061		do		231,533	United States, England, and Italy	142,412
	Rye	2,922	20,666		do		8	France	6
	Oats	76,172	9,270,831	301,273	do	559,484	92,070	....do	80,252
1879	Wheat	3,160,062	15,109,363	2,191,675	do	4,192,078	77,038	France, Russia, and Italy	143,589
	Barley	3,292,335	20,068,730	1,752,300	do	2,548,888	283,690	...do	239,653
	Maize	49,132	246,787		do		201,833	Malta, Asia, Turkey, France, and Austria	142,412
	Rye	1,783	14,844	18	do	18	618	France	405
	Oats	72,007	642,002	266,758	do	494,717	68	...do	58
1880	Wheat	6,095,337	44,017,349	2,924,940	do	5,594,615	33,839	France and Tunis	58,513
	Barley	3,527,817	22,150,180	2,490,266	do	3,022,148	21,023	France and Tunis	17,810
	Maize	40,358	277,109		do		28,350	France and United States	15,650
	Rye	1,825	17,077		do		1,432	France	938
	Oats	71,287	1,061,846	443,951	do	823,628	692	...do	583

UNITED STATES CONSULATE,
Algiers, July 24, 1882.

ALEX. JOURDAN, Consul.

O

www.ingramcontent.com/pod-product-compliance
Lightning Source LLC
Chambersburg PA
CBHW031453270326
41930CB00007B/983